Trinity Episcopal Miss
June 1951

Protestant Church Building

Protestant Church Building

Planning ⁌ Financing ⁌ Designing

By

WILLIAM H. LEACH

ABINGDON-COKESBURY PRESS
New York ● *Nashville*

PROTESTANT CHURCH BUILDING

COPYRIGHT, MCMXLVIII
BY STONE & PIERCE

PRINTED IN THE UNITED STATES OF AMERICA

Preface

PROTESTANT church building in the United States is characterized by two considerations. More church buildings are being planned now than at any other time in our history. The figures which are being released are almost astronomical. The second thing which is interesting and significant is that a new originality is being displayed by architects and churchmen. Protestant churches are definitely cutting away from the traditions of the past and are building for new utility and service.

To report these tendencies is important and is the object of this book. Being neither an architect nor an engineer, I am not undertaking to tell what churches should do. Instead, as a clergyman and editor, I am telling what churches are doing, and how they are going about it. This type of book may after all render the greatest service to the churches.

This book is planned to encourage churchmen to think seriously and to plan intelligently when they enter into building programs. If a few churches are led to provide better houses of worship through the reading of this volume, I will be satisfied.

A glossary of common architectural terms and of names of various furnishings for the church, a bibliography of good books on the different phases of church building, and a number of pictures and drawings which illustrate points made herein are included in the book.

WILLIAM H. LEACH

Contents

Illustrations

PART ONE
PLANNING AND FINANCING

Chapter I

We Need a New Church

BUILDING a new church is a serious matter. It takes a great deal more than looking at pictures and wishing. It means the raising of very substantial sums of money. It probably means the placing of a mortgaged indebtedness on the church which will burden it for years. It can be accomplished only if the membership works together in loyalty. There will be many nerve-trying experiences in the process. Christian tolerance, business acumen, and interchurch co-operation must go hand in hand.

There are many reasons why churches feel that they must build. The reasons usually fall into some of these general classes:

1. The present building is considered inadequate.
2. The people have moved to a new community.
3. A new church must be organized to meet population trends.
4. The new emphases on worship and education have made a new building desirable.
5. Social and economic changes in the community have made a building suitable for a new program essential.
6. The church has received a gift or bequest which must be expended in a building.

Once the idea has become vocal, there starts a long process of education, planning, and co-operation before the first

13

spadeful of earth is turned. A church building program needs the full support of the church, so a long process of education is necessary. In most communities there has been established an interchurch program. Other churches in the community need to be recognized. If the city or county has a church federation, definite rules have been set up for the guidance of churches which plan to build. The man who first says, "We need a new church," may not be conscious of the breadth of the program which he has started. It is not something to be entered into lightly.

PRELIMINARY STEPS

Let us follow through from the first vision to see just what a church should do, step by step, once the idea of building has been expressed.

First, it will try to determine why it needs a new building. We will assume that in this particular instance the reason is that expressed in the second item in the preceding list. The church feels that its future lies in a new community to which many of its members have moved. A Christian church should be very sure that it no longer can serve the present community before it decides to move. If it does reach that conclusion, then it may go ahead with plans for building in the new site.

Before it can discuss the matter intelligently, it will need to know what other churches are in the new community and what churches plan to build there. If the location is in a city organized for interchurch work, it is quite possible that the federation office can give this information immediately.

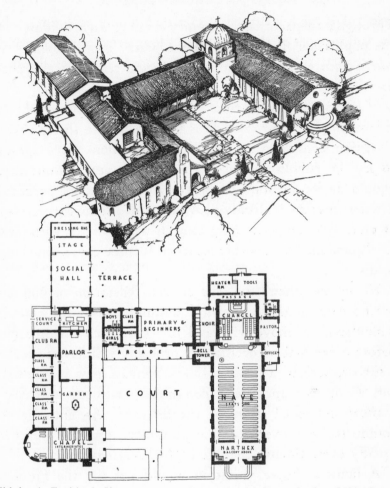

Nicholas A. Tomich, Architect   By courtesy of James Comfort Smith, Pastor

An Unusual Building
Community Church, Carmichael, Calif.

This interesting church is built of adobe brick, waterproofed with
a petroleum product known as "bitumul." Bricks were made by
young people of the church on the premises. They worked out in
this way their pledges to the building fund.

Through its department on comity it can give a breakdown of the population figures and offer a pretty good prophecy as to the future of the community. It will tell what churches have been given prior consideration.

"Comity" is a word that is unfamiliar to some people. It means simply "courtesy." It is used to denote the spirit of Christian consideration which denominations have agreed to use in establishing new churches in any community. Should the local committee on comity feel that the proposed new community is already provided with a sufficient number of churches, the petitioning church will want to withdraw its request and seek another location. It is the courteous thing to do.

If, on the other hand, the church federation or council has no data on the proposed community, then the church which seeks to move will need to secure such information before it can make a decision. It probably will have to make a survey, perhaps a house-to-house canvass. Few individuals can accurately appraise a community without a mathematical and social study of the territory. An enthusiastic committee may overvalue a community, just as a preacher usually overestimates the size of his congregation.

A house-to-house visitation should not list the families merely by church preferences. It is important that the age groups be given. How else will a church know the proper balance between the worship and educational facilities. It is well also if the survey can give a fairly good estimate of the value of the homes, the incomes of the various families, and something of their social habits. The public utilities us-

16

ually have information on the developing communities which will be helpful. In many instances they have shared this information with churches.

Next, we must have the local educational and publicity program. This needs to be a two-pronged program. The church must be made to understand why it is moving to a new location. Then, also, it needs to be informed as to what constitutes a good church building. The educational process will start, of course, with the church boards. But it should not stop there. All groups in the church should have the data presented, so that they may know just what is proposed. Up to this time the church has not made any material obligations. We know of no reason why enthusiastic boards should not secure an option on suitable sites while awaiting a final decision on the matter of building.

Not everyone will appreciate the information which comes from the detailed surveys of a community. It is also amazingly true that many good church people do not have the proper standards for judging an adequate church building. If an architect draws a pretty picture of a church, they are interested. But they do not always go back of the picture to see what the plans will offer. Leaders in the church need visual instruction to prepare their minds for any building program.

Practical visual instruction for this purpose involves the use of lantern slides, which may be secured from one of the denominational agencies or the Interdenominational Bureau of Architecture.[1] This agency, under the leadership of Dr.

[1] 297 Fourth Avenue, New York 10, N. Y.

17

Elbert M. Conover, offers a valuable consultative service on church building. Some of its publications are included in the bibliography at the back of this volume. Your denomination, and others, also are issuing valuable material on church building, techniques of organization for building, and terms of denominational loans.

Perhaps there is no method more productive of good in visual education than to persuade your membership to visit churches which have adequate church buildings. The members then become conscious of the changes in the chancel and worship appointments which have been taking place during the past generation. They see the individual class-rooms now considered essential, the departmental assemblies, the modern kitchen and dining-room facilities, and are then in a better position to judge the type of church which they will need.

SELECTION OF A LOT

If the church is to be built in a new location, the purchase of the building lot will normally be done by the church before a building committee is appointed. The selection of site needs careful consideration. The most desirable kind of lot is not always available. Architects have shown amazing skill in adapting buildings to whatever land is available, but the following features are desirable and should be sought:

1. The lot should be of sufficient size to accommodate the proposed building, to give parking space for automobiles, and to have an area about the completed structure for lawn,

From *Colonial Meeting Houses of New Hampshire*, Eva A. Speare

An Early
New England Church

*Sandown Meeting House
Sandown, N. H.*

This old New England Church
dates back to 1774. The upper
view shows the front balcony,
from which seats were re-
moved for the organ. Back of
the organ are the balcony pews,
for which elders paid extra
money. There restless children
could be shut from the eyes of
the minister. Below is the
goblet pulpit, common in early
New England churches.

air, and atmosphere. Many city building codes now make parking space essential to a building permit.

2. It should be near the geographical center of the parish. Studies have shown that interest in the work of the local church has a definite relationship to proximity. This is especially true for the church school.

3. It should be near public transportation. Not everyone possesses an automobile. Many churches have been handicapped during the war years by being off bus and streetcar lines. This requirement may be qualified by the addition of a caution that the building be far enough from the street that the street car and automobile noises will not interfere with the services of worship.

4. When the church is built on a lot even with or higher than the street level, a more commanding appearance is secured. Usually a lot which slants downward from the street is less effective than one which slants the other way.

5. The lot should be deep enough so that it is not necessary to build to the sidewalk. Impressiveness is gained by an expanse of lawn leading to the entrance.

The third step should be the appointment of a building committee. The preliminary steps can be carried on without such a committee, and they may develop individuals who show a special aptitude for this service. The building committee should not have the added burden of selling the idea of the new church. Instead, it takes up its burden when the church has been sold on the idea and devotes its energies to the processes of making the dream come true.

A good building committee should be representative of

the entire church. Its size may be determined by the size of the congregation. Much of its work may be done by assignment, but each church organization should feel it has a part in the building program. The committee has only such rights as are conferred upon it by the church. Usually it is given the authority to contract with an architect and builder, but no committee should consider it has such rights unless they are clearly set forth.

The specific task of the building committee is to study plans of churches, employ an architect, make contracts in the name of the church with the builders, and see that the building is properly erected. It will also have the direction of the program of public relations which publicizes the project to the local congregation and the community at large. Sometimes, but by no means as a matter of principle, the financial plans for the new building are also left in the hands of the building committee. This, however, is a large and important task, and it is usually desirable to make the financial campaign the responsibility of another committee.

Wise church leaders will appreciate that a building committee will do its work most effectively if the groundwork has been well laid. The committee has a difficult task at best. It has a right to expect that the church has decided a building should be erected, and that it is ready to furnish moral and financial support. When it has this assurance, it is fortified to begin its real work.

CHAPTER II

Organizing the Building Committee

THE first two considerations for a building committee were given in the preceding chapter. It is well to stress them again. First of all the committee should be representative. Everybody should be interested in the new church. It is to be the church of the trustees, the Sunday school, the ladies' aid society, the Boy Scouts, and of every other organization. So in the appointment of members every functional organization of the church should be recognized. In the larger churches it may seem that this will create a rigid organization. In actual practice the serious work will be assigned to a small executive committee of three or five persons. But it is necessary that the building committee represent the church, and that it keep close to the church during all of its work.

The second most important item is that the building committee should know just what the church expects it to do. Some churches appoint a building committee too early, when there has been no preparation for the step. Other churches fail to understand the specific duties and responsibilities which are assigned to the committee. Without giving it proper authority a church may expect a committee to enter into contracts and decide legal questions.

The two important procedures, once a church has decided on a new building, are: first, the appointment of the building committee to study church architecture and organize the construction of such a building; and, second, the appointment of the committee on finance which will have the task of seeing that the necessary funds are available. It may be desirable in some situations to combine the work under one committee. That is all right if it is understood. A building committee should know just what the church expects it to do.

In some instances the committee will be appointed by the congregation; in others, the official board will have the authority to appoint. But keep in mind that there are some responsibilities which cannot be delegated. A building committee may be able to use pledges as collateral to borrow money, but it never has authority to mortgage the church property. That power rests in the official board or the duly elected officers of the church. A committee may buy or sell property in the name of the church, but the proper church body must authorize the act. All property deeds must be in the name of the church, or its trustees, according to the laws of the state in which it exists.

THE ORGANIZATION

The building committee will need a chairman, a secretary, and a treasurer. If the responsibility of fund raising is given to this committee, it will need to appoint at once from its members a good committee on finance. In this instance, in addition to a recording and corresponding secretary it

23

will need a financial secretary and treasurer to work with the financial committee.

There will be need of other committees from time to time. Probably the needs can be as well met by special committees for particular projects as by standing committees which are to be appointed at the organization meeting. For instance, a special committee might be appointed to confer with suggested architects; another might have the responsibility of visiting certain churches to study special features; a third could be entrusted with the selection of an organ, and so on. In as much as it is difficult to anticipate all of the activities of the building committee, it is probably wise to assign tasks to special committees as the need may arise rather than set up standing committees. This is usually considered good executive strategy in the functioning of any temporary department or organization.

While the members of the building committee will represent the various functional groups of the church, it is well if they also will represent various activities of life. There is a place on the committee for the man who has had experience in talking with bankers. There is need for someone who has had legal training. There must be members who represent the various trades and can judge the quality of the work which is going into the building. Individuals who are sensitive to the history of the Christian church and the development of the religious arts also are needed. The ideal building committee will be a composite of these types of people.

24

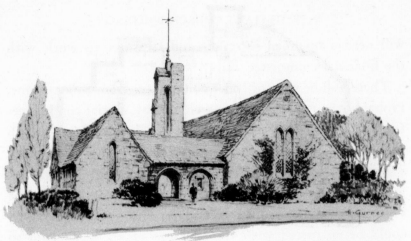

A STONE CHURCH

Portland Methodist Church, Portland, Tenn.

This church has a court between the nave and the small chapel.
The social hall is beneath the nave.

COMMITTEE'S FIRST TASK

The very first task to be taken up by the committee is
the study of church architecture. It is well if the congregation understands the qualities of a good church building. It
is necessary that the committee know them. Of course a
committee may go to an architect and say, "Design for us
a church." But the logical way is to take to the architect
some suggestions from the committee as to the type of
church it needs.

This training in church architecture can be secured from
books and leaflets which are available, from visits to
churches, and from consultation with men who know the
field. The bibliography in this book will be helpful. The

25

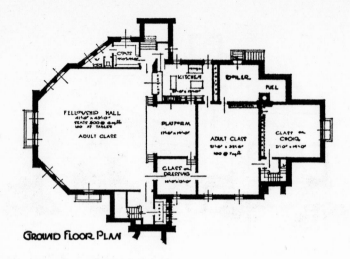

GROUND FLOOR PLAN

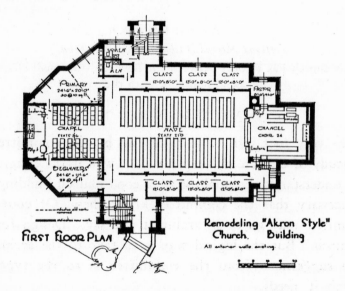

FIRST FLOOR PLAN

Remodeling "Akron Style"
Church. Building

All exterior walls existing.

CONVERTING THE AKRON PLAN

First Congregational Church, Kane, Penn.

The once popular Akron Plan is no longer in good favor. Here are some suggestions for remodeling, but it is a difficult task.

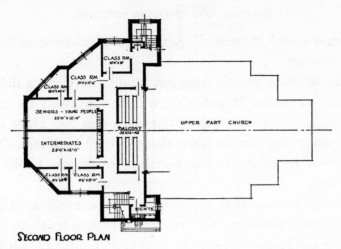

SECOND FLOOR PLAN

E. M. Conover, Consultant

Wenner & Fink, Architects

titles which have been starred are practical books which laymen will understand.

This study in church architecture will also include corre-
spondence with the denominational agency, which is a
clearing house for ideas. In most of the denominations there
is such an agency. It is usually found in the department of
home missions. Many churches plan to borrow money or
secure outright gifts from the denomination to aid them
in their building programs. It is well to know that when such
aid is anticipated the denominational agency will insist
on having something to say about the new building and its
cost. Others than the committee members should understand this. The information should be given any architect
who may afterward be employed. Suggested plans may be
secured from the denominational bureaus. The committee
will probably want to secure information from the Inter-

27

denominational Bureau of Architecture, mentioned in the first chapter.

This learning process need not be scheduled for a definite number of weeks. It probably will be continued for many months as the work of the committee goes on. There is always something new to learn about church buildings. Other steps will be taken as the members study the books and diagrams.

Almost as soon as it is organized, the committee will do well to get expressions from the various members about what their organizations expect in a church building. What do the women expect in a new church? They will expect a good kitchen and adequate dining room facilities. What do the educational leaders expect? They are sure to want departmental assemblies and individual classrooms. What do the young people wish? Perhaps they need a comfortable meeting place with a handy kitchenette. What do the choir members have in mind? They may want a robing room and, perhaps, a soundproof room for rehearsals. And so on. These expressions will be made without regard to actual funds which may be available. The "suit must be cut according to the cloth." But the workers in the departments of church work know better than anybody else what is best suited to their work. These ideas will be assembled and used in discussion with the architect.

CAPACITY OF THE CHURCH

Perhaps the next thing the church needs to know is the number of people it is to serve. How many people are found in the church service on Sunday morning? List the departments of the church school to see the number of persons in each one. How many usually attend the men's club, the young people's society, and the other group meetings? Will the church grow during the next ten years? If there is assurance of that, the building should be built in proportion to this expected increase. However, one of the most common mistakes in church building is to assume that a new building means inevitable growth. A building alone will not assure growth. If it is accompanied with a substantial debt, it may actually retard growth in the adult departments.

I have never seen a sure formula for measuring the future progress or retrogression for a church. The war, of course, has upset many prophecies. But before the war it was the depression. Just ahead is the period of reconstruction. Who is wise enough to see all of the factors which will influence church life? It is, however, the responsibility of the building committee to give such information to the architect. He will design the building in accordance with the figures that are given him.

"Don't build a church for the Easter congregation," has been said so often that it is hackneyed. But it is still true. Inasmuch as a committee can do so, it should invest the money of the church in a building suited to its membership. A church building should be individually tailored. One church will have more adults for the worship service than children in the church school; in another the situation may be reversed.

29

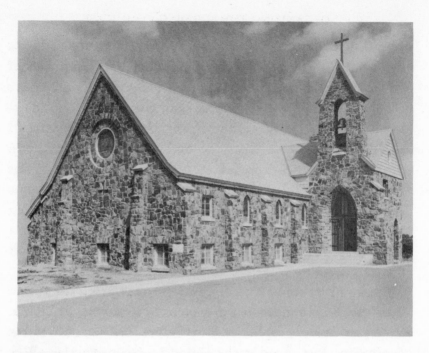

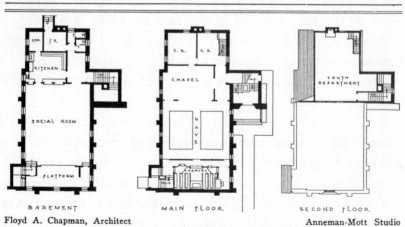

Floyd A. Chapman, Architect   Anneman-Mott Studio

BEAUTY IN A SMALL CHURCH
Centenary Methodist Church, Hamlin, Penn.
Native field stone was used for the walls.

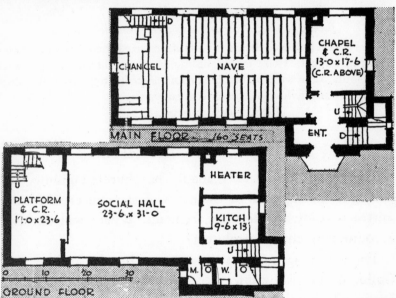

Barber & McMurry, Architects

SMALL CHURCHES CAN BE BEAUTIFUL

Memorial Methodist Church, Corryton, Tenn.

This little church is one of the best arguments we have that small churches need not be ugly.

Wenner & Fink, Architects
Elbert M. Conover, Consultant

By courtesy of William H. Neebe, Pastor

A Medium-sized Church

Bethany United Presbyterian Church, Bloomfield, N. J.

This is a well balanced design for a medium-sized church with a limited building budget. There is a doubling of the children's chapel with other units. Low walls and sloping roof reduce heating costs. Worship, education, and fellowship, each has emphasis.

(Floor plans on opposite page.)

SELECTING AN ARCHITECT

Having informed itself about the church building, and having a fair appraisal of the needs of the church, the committee is ready to select an architect. Where will one find a competent church architect?

There is a group known as the Church Architectural Guild. As far as I know, it is the only organization of experienced church architects. It is a small group, and by no stretch of imagination can its members expect to serve the many churches which today seek architectual help. Many architects who have never designed churches now have such assignments. An honest architect who will make a serious

32

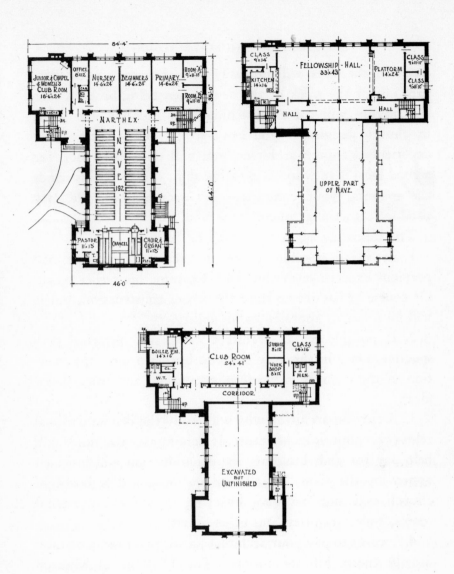

study of the work will probably do satisfactory work. Perhaps out of the work of the newer men being brought into the picture will come something very much worth while in church designs. If you can't secure the services of an experienced church architect, you will do well to look for a good local man who has creative ability. Place in his hands the material your committee has accumulated. He may produce something splendid for you.

The following suggestions may be helpful:

1. If at all possible secure an architect who has had previous experience in this field. Examine his earlier work. Of course he has grown since the earlier construction, but it will give you an appraisal of his ability.

2. If possible get an architect who has a historical perspective. Only in this way can you have a proper appreciation of the changes in worship, education, and recreational ideas.

3. Secure an architect who will study the denominational releases on church architecture. If denominational funds will help pay for your building, the denomination will insist on approving the plans. Your home mission board or board of church extension has some exacting ideas for educational rooms, toilet facilities, and other items.

4. Expect to pay your architect an adequate fee. Cut rates usually mean inferior service. The Division of Church Erection of the United Lutheran Church in America recommends a fee of 10 per cent when the total cost of construction is $15,000 or less; 8 per cent on work between $15,000 and $25,000; 6 per cent on all larger programs.

34

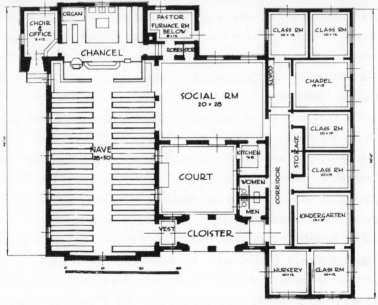

Barber & McMurry, Architects

A SPANISH MISSION STYLE CHURCH

First Methodist Church, Clewiston, Fla.

Note the social room, which offers accommodations for overflow congregations.

5. Look for a man who is temperamentally qualified to work with your committee, and with the contractors who will construct and complete the building.

Oftentimes there will be a good architect among the members of the church. He may be the logical man for the task. Experience has shown that when one of the church members is so employed it should be on a straight professional basis. He will make his personal contribution toward the new church. Do not expect him to lower the fee, which is based on the value of his professional work.

The architect who is retained will prepare the preliminary designs. They will be handed to the committee, who in turn will discuss the various features. Changes will be made to conform with suggestions. Gradually the entire building will be blueprinted and specifications prepared. Estimates of the cost will be made by the architect. When the plans are finally accepted, the time has come for the consideration of bids by the various builders. The architect provides each of these builders with blueprints and specifications. At the appointed time the bids are opened by the architect in the presence of someone designated by the committee.

The building contract varies. Some churches will give a single contract to include the building, pews, chancel fittings, and other furnishings. Others issue one contract to the general builder, and then reserve for other contracts installations such as pews. The organ is usually a special contract. Furniture and movable items seldom are in the original contract.

The contract with the architect provides for a partial

payment of his fee when the preliminary plans are completed. This might be 20 per cent. An additional payment is made when the bids are opened. This will be a larger percentage than was the first amount; 40 per cent may be an average. The balance is paid month by month as the work progresses.

The building contract also provides for payments according to the work which has been done. Payment is made each month on certification by the architect, and 85 to 95 per cent is the usual figure allowed. When the final work has been completed, the builder will have to provide a waiver of any liens against the property. Then thirty days after acceptance of the work he is entitled to the remainder.

SPECIAL SERVICES

During the erection of a new building there are opportunities for three attractive services. These are the breaking of the ground, the laying of the cornerstone, and the dedication of the completed structure.

The first is the simplest service. A spadeful of earth is turned at the point indicated by the builder or architect, and the ground is consecrated.

The cornerstone is placed at the most conspicuous corner of the building. On the face of the stone is the name of the church and the date of the erection. It has been hollowed out, and inside are placed various documents and items which will be of interest in later years. Items such as a history of the church, pictures of pastors and founders, Bibles, hymnbooks, and a few coins may be included.

The service of dedication is the greatest service of the three. At this service the keys of the building may be turned over by the chairman of the building committee to the proper church official. This signifies the completion of the work of the committee.

Proper promotion of each of these services will bring many worshipers. The finance committee will find these splendid occasions for getting cash contributions or for the securing of additional pledges.

Chapter III

Approaching the Financial Campaign

IT costs money to build a new church. It is easy for an enthusiastic congregation to overestimate its prospects for future growth and build much beyond its financial resources. There may have been a time when a bright new building, in itself, was assurance that people would flock to fill the pews. Such has not been the case in the last generation. People have considered carefully before joining a church with a heavy mortgage on its hands. As a result there have been many churches, even in prosperous communities, which have found the church mortgage a heavy handicap to their work. This error in estimation of prospects has been particularly common in many churches locating in rich city suburbs, where they have found that they were much too optimistic about the possibilities of future growth.

Mr. John G. Gredler of the Presbyterian (U.S.A.) Board of National Missions has studied many churches which have been burdened with mortgages. From his observations he has worked out a table which, barring unusual instances, probably gives a basis for estimating the amount which any local church should spend for a new building. He says that a church may feel safe when investing in such a project an amount equal to seven times its annual budget. Thus, if your church has an annual budget of $5,000, you may feel safe in spending $35,000 for a new building. Of this money four sevenths should be in hand at the beginning of the construction. The rest may be financed by a mortgage or other type of loan. These figures are, of course, less than many churches have spent in the past and are planning to spend at the present time, but Mr. Gredler insists that a study of 5,000 cases reveals that when churches spend more than the percentages suggested they are running into financial danger. If a church feels that its prospects for future growth are so bright that it will need greater facilities, it would be well to work out a plan for progressive construction. In this way a church may be enlarged as the parish grows, and the large burden of a great building is not placed on a small congregation. This suggestion may be doubly worth while when building costs are high. No one can say with assurance that prices will be lower, but there is always the possibility. There is little doubt that there will be improved ideas in construction for church purposes which will be available if a church delays some of its units pending growth.

ORGANIZATION OF A BUILDING CAMPAIGN

The organization and execution of a campaign for building funds is a task of considerable proportions. As the amount to be raised is several times that of the annual budget, the usual procedure of the every-member canvass would seem to be insufficient. To start with, the committee will

40

have to make a decision as to whether it will plan and direct the effort, or whether it will bring into the community a professional fund raiser. There are arguments in favor of both methods.

Among the many firms and individuals who offer their services as leaders in the financial effort, there are consecrated men who have the cause of the church at heart. At the same time they have a wealth of experience in methods, which is very valuable. Their counsel, available to a church when it is planning the campaign, may be very important. They are able to appraise the financial resources of a congregation much better than a local person. They are usually paid a fee based on the total amount of money raised.

The minister is an important man in the financial effort. If professional leadership is not secured, he will be forced into fund-raising activities. Much of it will be alien to him. Tensions created during the campaign many times have limited the minister's influence. The old adage that when a minister has built a new church it is time for him to move probably has its basis in this fact. Professional leadership can shield him from many of the difficult things of a campaign.

On the other hand there is a danger of criticism if a church calls in a professional to direct the work. There are some people who will feel that any money paid for such leadership might better go into the building. If local leadership and resources are available so that the funds can be raised easily, it is an indication of strength to have the whole thing done by the local church.

The tendency in church fund raising today, especially

where large amounts are concerned, is to employ good fund-raising counsel. The criticism of cost is easily answered. The average church will raise much more money under such leadership so the fee paid does not come out of the proposed building.

If professional help is employed, the church will find that each leader has evolved his own method of procedure. He will want this followed in every particular. What is said in the rest of this chapter is in no sense to be considered as the outline of a program for any fund raiser. I am simply offering suggestions to the churches which decide to conduct their own campaigns. We will take up the items one by one.

SETTING UP A CAMPAIGN

1. *The Creation of a Building Fund.*—The origin of the building fund may date years before the actual construction of the building. It may start with a gift by a generous individual. More likely the women's organization has begun a fund for that purpose. Others may add to it. If the church faces no financial emergencies which dissipate the fund in the payment of annual expenses, a considerable amount may be on hand when the time comes for actually starting the new building.

A few churches—there are altogether too few of these—try to write an amount in the annual budget for a new building. There is a constant depreciation in any church building. If that could be balanced by an equal amount of money laid aside for a building fund, the erection of a

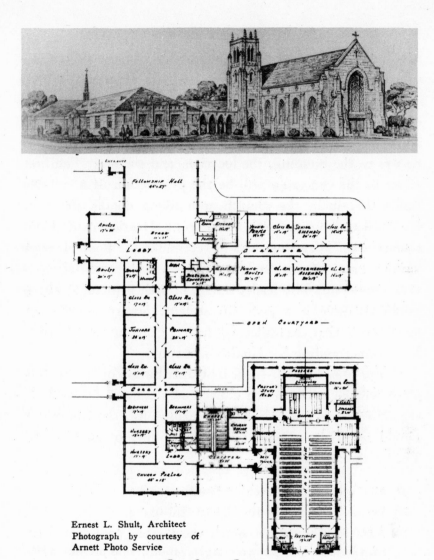

Ernest L. Shult, Architect
Photograph by courtesy of
Arnett Photo Service

ONE-STORY CHURCH
Grace Methodist Church, Goose Creek, Tex.

This pleasing design is all on one floor. It is possible where large lots
are available. There is, in addition, plenty of open courtyard space,
which can be converted into a parking area.

new building when needed would be easily financed. Preconstruction financing is a luxury few churches enjoy.

2. *Preliminaries of the Campaign.*—The actual starting of the financial campaign will await the decision to build and the employment of an architect. There must be definiteness as to the building, the location, and the cost. The first effort in the campaign will be the production of a suitable leaflet describing the church and giving details about it. It is well to have pictures of the front elevation made from the architect's drawings and to reproduce the floor plans of various parts of the building. This visual presentation is very important. This leaflet should be well printed. A cheap publicity piece is a poor investment. Secure a sufficient quantity, so that the leaflet will have a generous distribution. Keep type standing for further printings.

3. *The Mailing List.*—The first distribution of the mailing piece will be through the church services and by mail. If the church does not have a good mailing list, the committee should set itself at once to the compiling of such a list. The list should include:

a) Members of the church by families.

b) Former members of the church still living.

c) Adult members of the church school, young people's societies, men's clubs, and women's organizations, who are not members of the church.

d) The Sunday school enrollment by classes.

e) Nonmember citizens who might be considered good prospects for gifts to the new church.

APPROACHING THE FINANCIAL CAMPAIGN

All of these names will of course be accompanied by correct addresses. If an addressing machine is available, the names may be placed on stencils. In the case of church members only the head of the family will need to be on the stencil.

The leaflet carrying the information about the church should be sent to groups *a, b, c, and e* of the list. It is usually safe to assume that the children in the Sunday school will belong to families represented in the other lists. The mailing of the leaflets will probably produce some gifts. Its immediate purpose, however, is to convey the idea that the church is definitely planned. The matter of arousing an interest in the new building should come before the solicitation of funds.

4. *Analysis of the Resources for Building.*—This is one of the tasks of the committee which will not be publicized. Many people have an objection to a listing of their resources and annual incomes. However, the government knows; the banker knows; the credit organization knows. It is not as difficult as one may at first suppose to list such assets on a card.

For instance, the wages paid craftsmen are fairly uniform. If a man is an automobile mechanic in your community, you know what his hourly wage is and the number of hours he normally works. You know the salaries paid to teachers and public officials. It is more difficult to estimate the incomes of men in business for themselves. Your figures do not need to be minutely accurate. But it is going to be a help to know just what percentage of the income per year is going to be necessary per member in order to pay for the new church

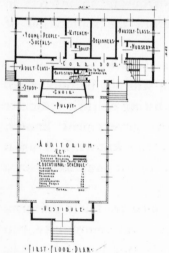

Department of Church Architecture   Baptist Sunday School Board, Nashville, Tenn.

THE OLD RENEWED

Antioch Baptist Church, Jarratt, Va.

It looks like a new church. But it still uses the old building, which
has become the worship unit, with education rooms added.

building. That does not mean that assessments are going to be made. Many will give more than their share. But it does mean that very early in the campaign you will know whether or not it is going to be a success.

Assume a congregation of two hundred families with a total estimated annual income of $500,000. The budget of such a church will probably run from $10,000 to $15,000, which is 2 or 3 per cent of the total income. We are talking mathematics, not stewardship, here. There are very few congregations which give a tenth of their combined incomes. If a tithe were given in the above instance, the local church budget would be $50,000. That just is not in the books.

Taking Mr. Gredler's figures and applying them to the above congregation, we see that this church can safely build at a cost of $70,000, providing $40,000 is in hand by the time the building is dedicated. This would leave $30,000 to be pledged in a campaign. If pledges are to be paid in weekly, monthly, or quarterly installments over a period of three years, each member would need to give the church just double the amount he is now pledged to give during that period of time. If the $40,000 is not available, it will mean the average member must give more than double his usual annual gift on the three-year basis.

To keep to easier figures let's assume that the church must raise $50,000 in pledges. That is 10 per cent of the annual estimated income of the members. If a man has an annual income of $10,000, his pledge to the new church should be $1,000, payable over a period of time. If the annual income is $1,500, the fair gift might be $150.

47

None of these figures are for publicity purposes. They will not be used openly for solicitation purposes. But they are developed to instruct the building committee that it may properly see its resources and, also, that individual members may see their own responsibility for giving.

For instance, assume that the man with the $10,000 annual income is on the committee. As he goes over the figures which are being produced, he knows very well that a pledge of $100 or $200 is entirely too low for a man of his income. The chairman of the committee can easily point out that unless the committee members make pledges commensurate with their incomes they are hardly in a position to ask others to pay their share.

A professional fund raiser of my acquaintance works out his table of income and responsibility in front of the building committee. He uses a blackboard. When he has completed his analysis, he asks the committee members frankly if they are willing to contribute their share. If they accept their responsibility, he knows that the effort will be a success; if they refuse to do so, he knows that the amount will not be reached. The campaign succeeds or fails in that meeting.

This preliminary activity is very important. The amount which a church can put into a new church building is determined by the financial resources of its congregation and the benevolent spirit of those to be solicited. Many of the heartaches of churches which have carried burdensome mortgages for years have been caused by the failure to appraise their resources properly.

CHAPTER IV

Getting the Money

THE actual money which goes into a new church building comes from many sources. Very few churches are
limited to one method in raising funds. A good principle
is to test the various sources before making the membership-
wide campaign for the final gifts.

1. *Sale of Property.*—A large percentage of churches
which build have material assets from the sale of the old
estate. In case the church is moving from a business to a
residential section, the sale of the old real estate, its value
increased by the growing city, is a considerable factor.

2. *Bequests and Gifts.*—Many churches have funds which
have been created without an effort on their part. Wealthy
members have died leaving bequests for the church. The
money received in this way should go into permanent funds
for church building. There is always the possibility of gifts
for building purpose.

3. *Memorials.*—At the present time churches can secure
a considerable amount of the furnishings and equipment for
a new church through the acceptance of specific memorials.
The war has brought bereavement to many families. There
has always been a desire to memorialize individuals who have
been close to the church. This is intensified at the present

49

time. If in announcing plans for a new church a list of possible memorials is included, several—possibly many—will be offered.

The items which naturally lend themselves to the memorial idea include:

the chancel	crosses and candlesticks
altar or Communion table	windows
baptismal font	drinking fountain
organ	classrooms
chimes and bells	pulpit furniture

These all possess permanency and have aesthetic values. It is hard to visualize material equipment such as heating and ventilating systems as memorials. Carpets and rugs are too short-lived.

There have been churches which have capitalized the memorial idea to the point where each room, desk, pew, and chair has been used as a memorial. The memorial idea is a legitimate one. When, however, the effort is mechanized to the point of a pressure campaign, it loses much of its value.

4. *Denominational Assistance.*—Every local church will want to canvass the possibility of aid from the denomination. Such aid is usually given through the home missions board. Fairly uniform standards have been set up. Denominational assistance is available in the form of outright gifts, loans without interest, and loans with a low rate of interest.

The purpose of the denominational assistance is to aid churches which would otherwise be unable to build. That does not mean, of course, that only small, poverty-stricken

THE BOOK OF REMEMBRANCE

All Saints Memorial Church, Providence, R. I.

The Book of Remembrance is one of the most
effective methods of stimulating gifts for permanent memorials as well as a most satisfactory
means of recording the names of donors. Not just
the givers of special memorials but those who
contribute to special permanent funds have a
place in these records. The repository and the
book are of highest quality, worthy of money
given for these purposes.

By courtesy of Whittemore Associates

churches are aided. Oftentimes strategic churches in promising centers receive aid because of their prospects. Any gifts or loans are made only after careful appraisal of the resources and the prospects of the church. Definite requirements are made as to the cost of the building and the amount which the local church must assume. Some denominational boards withhold all aid until architectural plans have been approved.

5. *Gifts from Benevolent-minded Individuals.*—There are still many people of wealth who like to give to religious work of which they approve. Gifts from such individuals have helped many churches in their time of need. These donors are not necessarily church members. A new York widow has an affection for a little church in a rural area where she went to Sunday school. The result is a substantial gift to the church. A successful businessman wants to perpetuate the family name by building a memorial church to his parents. A wealthy lover of music has given five pipe organs to five churches and will probably give more. A local businessman feels that his generosity should be extended to all of the churches in the community.

A definite effort should be made to secure such gifts. A committee on special gifts will have the very delicate task of creating the list and placing the request before these prospects. While a contact might be made by mail, much of the work of this committee will be by personal solicitation. Most men and women are easily approached by a committee from the home town, but occasionally someone is so well protected that it takes considerable ingenuity to secure the appointment for the interview.

In addition to individuals there are charitable foundations which have been established by men of wealth. In these foundations the task of studying and passing on request lies in the hands of secretaries. The tendency of recent years has been to discourage gifts to denominational enterprises. It is not at all a fertile field for local church gifts.

6. *Classes and Organizations.*—Many of the organizations of the church, including church school classes, plan to contribute to the new building. Some may have funds for the purpose that have been created through the years. These groups should be canvassed to see just what amounts they will pledge. Make it clear to such organizations that individual pledges will also be asked, so that they will clearly understand that there is a distinction between the organization pledge and the individual pledge. Adults should be discouraged from making their pledges to aid one of the church organizations rather than pledging directly to the fund. In the case of children giving by classes may take precedence over the individual giving.

THE CANVASS OF THE CHURCH MEMBERS AND FRIENDS

After the preliminary resources have all been analyzed and the church knows just how much money is available from these, the time has come for the congregation-wide solicitation. Keeping in mind the annual income of the congregation, the committee will determine whether the campaign is to be for cash gifts or pledges to be paid over a period of years. In most instances the amount is so great that time pledges will be made with the stipulation that they are for weekly, monthly, or quarterly payments. The period should not run too long. Eighteen months, two years, or at the most three years would be recommended. The economic conditions of the country rapidly change in these days. The best-intentioned individual may be without financial resources in a few months.

It is well to keep in mind that the number of members in a church is not the index of the amount of money which can be raised. The basis of computation is the financial resources of the congregation combined with the spirit of stewardship. A congregation with a high sense of stewardship will produce more than a larger one without it. The measure of this spirit may be found by estimating the percentage of the annual income which is contributed to the annual budget. Discussion of church giving based on the tithe has confused thinking on this point. If all Christians were tithers, there would be no need of extra campaigns for church buildings. A general statement to that effect, however, cannot disguise the fact that very few, if any, churches are so fortunately situated. Use the method discussed earlier in this book and see where your church stands in its program of giving.

The useful framework for an every-member canvass is a good one for this campaign. Not just members but friends, organizations, Sunday school classes, and all others in the list in Chapter III who have not been previously solicited should be included. Keep in mind that an every-member canvass is not an every-member canvass unless every prospect is given an opportunity to contribute.

No campaign should be started without sufficient preliminary educational and publicity work. This is usually necessary in the annual every-member canvass. It is particularly needed where the larger amount is involved. Let's take an illustration from the World War. The infantry was trained to go into the enemy's territory and force him to surrender. But first the enemy was softened by airplane raids, artillery barrage, and in many instances naval fire. Without this artillery, air, and naval support, the success of the infantry would have been impossible. The canvass committee is the infantry of the financial campaign. But its work is very difficult unless the barrage of publicity and education has been effective. The publicity pieces shown in this book will give an idea of how carefully churches have gone into this program to make the fund raising successful.

STEPS TO THE CAMPAIGN

1. *Selecting Solicitors.*—The weakness of any every-member canvass is that few churches can produce a sufficient number of solicitors who are effective salesmen for the church. The men or women you select will not all have the capacity you wish. You must prepare the way through publicity and make their task one of answering questions and of picking up the pledges.

2. *Training Solicitors.*—They should know about everything there is to know about the new building. They must be able to tell why the particular location was selected, what it is going to cost, and what educational facilities it will have. They will also know the ratio of giving necessary to reach the goal.

3. *Assigning Solicitors.*—A good rule is to have captains over each group of ten. This group should then be divided into five teams of two solicitors each. A team will work each geographical district.

4. *Securing the Pledges of the Solicitors.*—Each solicitor should make his pledge before he goes out to solicit others. Unless he has sold himself on the idea of the new church, he will not be of much value in the campaign.

5. *Dividing the Parish Into Districts.*—The easiest way, and the one which will prevent criticism of favoritism, is a geographical division. The solicitor need not serve in the district in which he lives. His own pledge, however, should be credited to his home district.

6. *Setting Goals for Each District.*—Since people have the tendency to group themselves by possessions, some geographical districts will have much larger possibilities than others. Set definite goals based on incomes for each district. The teams will make about the same number of calls. But common sense would indicate that ten calls on families in a laboring area cannot begin to approximate the total in pledges which would be possible in one of the wealthier residential areas. A discussion of the methods of finding the incomes and of estimating ability to give will be found in Chapter III.

7. *Planning the Solicitation.*—Give definite dates for the solicitation. While the annual canvass usually is confined to a single day, a building campaign need not be so limited.

8. *Reporting on Progress.*—If the campaign extends over a number of days or weeks, have definite periods for reporting. List the reports on a blackboard or bulletin board so that the

PUBLICITY BOOKLETS

Attractive booklets which show the plans and purposes of the proposed new church are essential in a good publicity campaign.

entire congregation, if interested, may see how the work is progressing.

A good plan of listing of this is as follows:

District No.	Captain	Calls Assigned	Calls Made	Goals	Pledged	To Go
1	Cook	36	20	$2,100	$1,500	$ 600
4	Byron	33	18	3,000	1,800	1,200

Reports such as these kept constantly before the workers stimulate them to complete the task, and give a good estimate as to whether the goal will be reached.

The number of calls to be made by the teams should be fairly uniform. It is better to have a large number of solicitors with a smaller number of calls assigned than to have a small number of solicitors with a large number of calls to be made. Experience has shown that any group of solicitors will do better work if they are not given too many assignments.

VARIATIONS OF THE PLAN

While the foregoing gives a good picture of a good financial effort, it is not the only method which is possible. Some churches prefer to start the campaign with a mass meeting, accepting pledges at that meeting. Where this plan is used, the solicitors' first task is to make sure that their prospects are at the meeting. The cards are assigned in advance, and the first instructions given are to telephone or personally invite the prospects to be present at the mass meeting where their pledges will be solicited. Any pledges received at such meetings should be credited to the proper geographical unit.

A careful follow-up should be made of all prospects who are not present. The chart discussed above will still be used, but the first day will show a goodly amount of pledges in hand.

It is difficult to compare the merits of this big meeting plan with those of personal solicitation. Much depends upon the personality of the chairman or speaker at the meeting and the organization which has been perfected. Individual givers are the heart of success of any church campaign, and they must not be lost. If the pledges are solicited at a public meeting, it is well for the larger givers to be approached in advance and checked as to the size of their gifts. The weakness of the public meeting is that it may fail to put sufficient pressure on the potential larger contributors.

The training of the solicitors may take any one of several forms. Some churches plan meetings for several nights to discuss the details of the building program and the campaign. Many times series of luncheons give the opportunity for the indoctrination. An enthusiastic committee of canvassers will probably mean an enthusiastic response. This side of the effort needs to be emphasized in the planning.

CHAPTER V

Pledging, Paying, Accounting

THERE is no substitute for Christian stewardship. Many clever schemes for raising church money have been developed. Some churches have preferred to borrow from their members. There have been several types of financing through life insurance. We mention these, but as a principle they should not be used as long as it is possible to get actual gifts. First, seek outright gifts; second, seek emergency plans in the form of loans, insurance, and so forth.

The raising of substantial funds requires that the pledges be so arranged that they fit into the individual's financial habits. Most people today work for a weekly or semi-monthly wage; therefore, the easiest way for most people to pay is through a pledge which provides for weekly payments. The introduction of the weekly offering envelope was a mechanical thing, but it multiplied church giving when it was adopted. It is easy to understand that it is much more convenient to get a pledge of one dollar a Sunday for two years than to secure a pledge for a hundred dollars to be paid in thirty days.

However, experience has taught that it is not wise to have pledges run too long. Three years should be the outside limit; two years is much preferable. Some churches are having their pledges made for one year; then a canvass is made for the second year, and so on.

The Temple Baptist Church of Baltimore, Maryland, in raising a fund of $60,000 for a new addition, planned to collect the money over a four-year period. Pledges for the operating budget of the church are made prior to January 1, when the church year begins. The annual pledges to the building fund are made prior to July 1, when the church building year starts. Envelopes are given following each canvass. Thus the church member has two sets of envelopes, one for the operating expenses of the church and for benevolences, and the other for the church building fund. A more common practice is to insert monthly envelopes into a single package for the contributor. While the effort to raise $60,000 for the building has been spread over four years, a new solicitation is made each year. In this particular instance the plan of a campaign each year has been successful.

One very apparent asset of a plan such as this is that it permits each contributor to make a comparison immediately between the operating and benevolent budget and the church building budget. He can see without much effort the portion he should pledge toward the whole.

THE UNIT PLEDGE

Other churches prefer to make the appeal on the unit basis. Assume that fifty dollars is considered as a unit. The pledge card gives the opportunity to assume as many units as one feels wise. A typical pledge of this kind is that used by the Peoples Methodist Church, South Portland, Maine.

In consideration of the gifts of others and for the purpose of erecting a new church home for Peoples Methodist Church of South Portland, I hereby subscribe

———————— unit(s) at $100 each, payable monthly, within one year of date as follows:

—————————————————————————————————

Amount of cash with subscription $————————————

Signed ————————————————————————————

Address ————————————————————————————

(This pledge may be canceled because of illness or any other unavoidable circumstance.)

The reader should notice the cancellation line on the pledge above. This is a very wise provision. It encourages pledges. In case of ill health or financial reverses the church would not wish to press payment of the pledge anyway. The courts have consistently held that a pledge to a church building is legally collectible.

When the Methodist Church of Mount Lebanon, Pennsylvania, solicited for pledges to liquidate a $50,000 indebtedness, it found another provision of the pledge very productive. There was a general optimism that the fund would be oversubscribed. If this proved true, the committee agreed to refund to each contributor an amount proportionate to his individual gift to the entire fund. This clause of the pledge

Conrad, Hays, Simpson & Ruth, Architects   Photograph by R. Marvin Wilson

CLASSICISM IN ARCHITECTURE

St. Martin's Chapel, St. Paul's Episcopal Church, Cleveland Heights, Ohio

The classic lines of this small chapel
set it apart for worship and devotion.

SOLDIERS' CHURCHES

Above. A chapel built by natives of Guadalcanal in memory of their soldier friends slain in battle. *Below.* A soldier-built chapel at an undisclosed location. Note the use of gun shells in the construction.

read: "This subscription is made with the understanding that when the mortgage debt has been paid, there will be refunded to me, insofar as subscriptions permit, such portion of my payments hereunder as exceeds the average of all payments."

Some churches have found that pledging is encouraged if the pledge cards are offered in the form of bonds. One type of such bond contains coupons. Assume that the face of the pledge is one hundred dollars. This is to be paid in twenty monthly installments. A coupon is clipped each month and sent to the church with a check for five dollars. This plan is novel and offers a self-accounting system.

SECURITIES AS GIFTS

Most Americans acquired war bonds during the Second World War. The popular E Bond is increasing in value each year as it nears maturity. It may be possible to secure a substantial amount of money through the gift of these bonds and other securities.

It would be well for the church to have a committee to analyze and appraise securities and bonds which may be available. This committee may have also the task of helping the individuals sell the securities when that seems wise. The only way the E Bonds can be redeemed is by the individual. They cannot be transferred to churches or individuals. Gifts made in this way are eligible for exemption in the annual income tax statement up to 15 per cent of one's annual income.

SEGREGATION OF FUNDS

It is usually wise to segregate the building funds from other funds of the church. The financial secretary and treasurer should be selected and appointed for this particular task. The pledges should be transcribed to a book or cards, according to the system thought best for the church. The plan for collecting and accounting should not be unnecessarily complicated but must be sufficiently inclusive to enable the collection of the pledges.

A division of the pledges into the methods of payment is usually wise. The pledges which are to be paid in one sum at a given date require one kind of accounting; those pledged to quarterly payment will require a different method; most of the pledges will fall in the weekly or monthly class. If the division is made in the bookkeeping, some confusion will be avoided in the sending out of notices and the recording of payments.

The larger pledgers usually prefer single payment or quarterly payment of the pledges. Probably the best way where the single-payment pledges are concerned is to expect the payment on the date specified and, if it does not come, make a personal visit or telephone call as a reminder. The pledges scheduled for periodic payments should be listed in quarterly reports showing the amount pledged, the payments which have been made, and the payments which are now due.

The selection of any method for the accounting of the building fund need not be based alone upon the efficiency of the system. The most efficient system for a trained accountant may prove unsatisfactory where the work is being done by

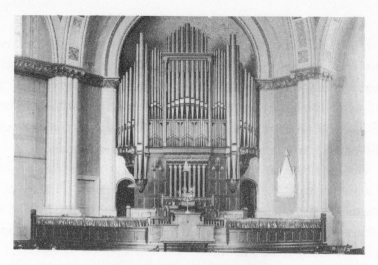

A DIVIDED CHANCEL

Erskine and American Church, Montreal

These "before and after" views show how one old church in Canada removed its organ pipes and built a divided chancel. The church is rich in symbolism, as may be seen in the small portion visible in these illustrations.

a volunteer. In the latter case a bound book is usually preferable to any visual card system, no matter how valuable the card system has proved under different circumstances. In the case of the larger churches which have well-equipped offices, visible card records keyed for easy reference and addressing stencils facilitate the notices and collections.

The safe rule in all church financing is to do everything one judiciously can to prevent pledges from falling into arrears. If the pledger gets behind in his payments, it may be difficult to get the money, and the church also faces the possibility of losing the member.

RAISING MONEY ON MORTGAGE

Desirable as it may be, very few churches are free from debt when opened for worship. The usual way of taking care of the indebtedness is by placing a mortgage on the church, pledging the real estate and buildings as security. If the church holds a sufficient number of good pledges, it is sometimes possible to borrow on these as security without the necessity of a mortgage.

There are several sources for mortgage money.

The church may seek to borrow the money from its own members. The face value of the mortgage may be divided up into bonds, and these sold to the members and friends of the church. They may be non-interest- or interest-bearing bonds with definite dates for payment on the face of the bond. Few churches have been able to sell the non-interest-bearing bonds, but more have been successful in disposing of bonds which carry a modest rate of interest. The greatest sales resistance to such bonds or notes is the feeling that the church is really seeking a gift, and that purchasers will be expected to turn the bonds over to the church. That is probably the reason why most churches prefer to go elsewhere for their loans.

The second source of mortgage money is the denominational church-erection board. These boards make a survey of the church and its possibilities and offer terms which the commercial bank cannot offer. They may lend part of the money without interest and part with interest. The board is seeking no profit by the extension of the work of the church.

A third source of money is the local bank. Most church mortgages are placed with the banks. There is always a moral situation involved where a church mortgage is concerned. Church property is seldom of such a nature that it can be easily converted to other uses. The bank in lending money on a church mortgage makes it a moral as well as a financial risk. It considers very carefully the names of the men who sign the mortgage notes for the church. As a rule the signers of the mortgage note sign as officers of the church and do not assume individual responsibility, but there have been instances in which the bank has asked endorsement of individuals before lending the money.

A fourth source of money for mortgages is the life insurance companies. Not all companies are interested in such loans. Probably there are fewer companies now considering church mortgages than there were a generation ago. But they are among the possibilities when a church is seeking money.

A few churches have taken hold of the annuity idea and

A. Hensel Fink, Architect

AN EFFECTIVE SMALL CHURCH
Church of God, Dundalk (Baltimore), Md.

This church offers an interesting study. It is a small church which seats 244 in the nave. It offers social and educational rooms, though curtains are used for some individual classes. A baptismal pool is at the east end of the chancel.

have financed their new church by issuing annuity bonds. These bonds, of course, pay annual amounts during the life of the holder. Upon his death all obligations stop. If the buyer of the annuity lives for years, the annual payments cut deeply into the principal, so that the church gets but little return for the money. The annuity plan is more adapted to those agencies which are in position to invest their funds. The payment of the annuity in such cases is offset by earnings of

70

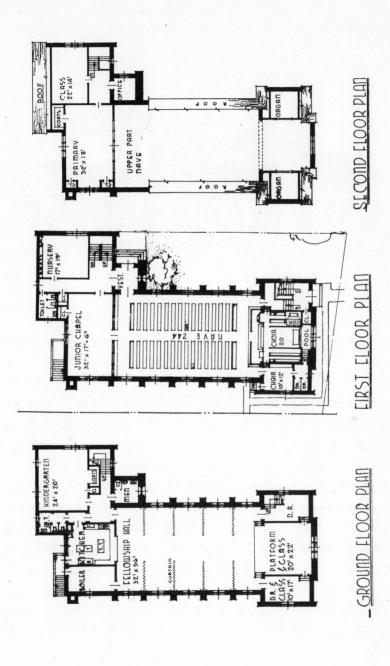

SECOND FLOOR PLAN

ROOF

CLASS
22' x 14'

OFFICE

COATS

PRIMARY
32' x 18'

UPPER PART
NAVE

ROOF

ROOF

ORGAN

ORGAN

FIRST FLOOR PLAN

TOILET

NURSERY
17' x 19'

CL

UP

VEST.

JUNIOR CHAPEL
32' x 17'-6"

NAVE 2-44

CHOIR
2-0

CHOIR
10' x 12'

POOL

DR.

GROUND FLOOR PLAN

KINDERGARTEN
24' x 20'

COATS

MEN

KITCHEN

BOILER

FELLOWSHIP HALL
32' x 56'

CURTAIN

D.R. &
CLASS
10' x 17'

PLATFORM
& CLASS
20' x 22'

D. R.

BUILDING ON A SLOPE

Lake Harriet Lutheran Church, Minneapolis, Minn.

This is a splendid example of modern designing to use on a sloping lot. By taking advantage of the natural geography the architects have assured natural light in the fellowship hall under the nave.

---

the principal. The local church is using its money to pay for new construction, so it is denied the earning protection enjoyed by agencies. One hesitates to recommend interest-bearing annuities to the average church.

Some of the larger churches have been financed by mortgage bond issues which have been floated by established bonding houses. Unless the mortgage indebtedness runs into several thousands of dollars, such financing is probably not available. As a matter of fact few bonding houses at the present time are interested in financing churches in this way.

Several insurance plans have been offered as a substitute for direct giving. They are usually somewhat as follows: The contributor makes a cash payment to the church. The church assumes the premium payments on a policy in which the contributor is the beneficiary. On maturity of the policy the contributor gets his money back from the insurance company. In one contract the church agrees to finance a policy which will bring the contributor, in thirty-five years, an amount one and one-half times as large as his original loan. In case of death the policy immediately gives the value of the policy to his family.

A church which is erecting a good building on valuable real estate, and which holds a goodly number of honest pledges, is in a good position to solicit mortgage money. However, it should make sure that its annual budget possibilities can care for the interest and make substantial payments on the principal.

LIQUIDATION OF THE INDEBTEDNESS

The church will be as much interested in the orderly liquidation of any mortgage indebtedness as in collecting on pledges. By far the best way is to provide in the annual budget of the church for an amount which will pay the interest and the principal as it may come due. A much less desirable way is to have periodic drives to "reduce the building debt." Such drives become difficult after a few repetitions. The building, no longer new, is hardly a basis for such an appeal. Churches should carefully consider in any building program their ability to meet in an orderly way the obligations which are undertaken.

May I suggest a rule which applies to personal indebtedness

73

as well as to corporate financial obligations. Many times we feel that credit is too difficult to obtain. It is hard to get the necessary cash. But remember this: No matter how difficult it may be to borrow money, it is always more difficult to pay it back.

PART TWO

BUILDING THE CHURCH

CHAPTER VI

Building for Worship

THE primary purpose of building a church is to enable men and women to approach God. Every other objective is subsidiary to this. No matter what social or educational facilities the building offers, if it fails to be a stimulus to prayer, it has failed in its purpose. The achievement of a building of worship involves the aspiration of religion and the techniques of many arts and trades. It is not alone the matter of the worship center or the chancel; the entire building, exterior and interior, should share in the message. The lot which is selected, the type of architecture, the appearance of the lawn, the approaches to the building, as well as the interior appointments, are important.

The statement by A. L. Drummond in his book *The Church Architecture of Protestantism* puts this splendidly in a single paragraph.

The wayfarer who passes a church, even if he does not enter, should experience in some measure a feeling of release and liberation from the pettiness of daily life that will help him to see everything in a truer perspective. The church should be "the outward and visible sign of inward and spiritual grace," the infinite realized in a little space, and conversely, a personal place of refuge carved out of infinity.[1]

[1] (New York: Charles Scribner's Sons, 1935), p. 185.

AN ALTAR FOR STUDENTS
Protestant Chapel
United States Military Academy, West Point, N. Y.

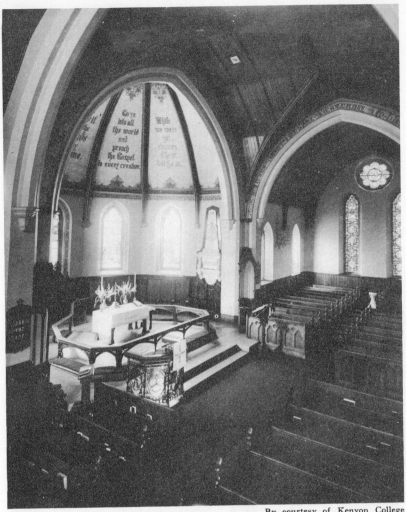

A COMMUNION TABLE FOR STUDENTS

Church of the Holy Spirit, Kenyon College, Gambier, Ohio

An Episcopal church with a Communion table is unusual in these days. But in many parts of the United States in earlier years there was prejudice against the use of altars. This church was constructed in that period in the diocese of Ohio.

A Church with Colonial Lines

St. Christopher's-by-the-River Gates Mills, Ohio

This Colonial design in the Western Reserve maintains the spirit of old New England.

A Remodeled Colonial Church

First Congregational Church Branford, Conn.

Here is an example of a remodeled Colonial church. A divided chancel with altar takes the place of the center pulpit. The interior preserves the clean, severe pattern of Colonial architecture.

From a water color by John Edward Miller. Photograph by R. Marvin Wilson.

By courtesy of Whittemore Associates

From *Colonial Meeting Houses of New Hampshire*, Eva A. Speare

A Bullfinch Interior

Lancaster, Mass.

This view shows the skill of Charles Bullfinch in the beautiful pulpit with hangings and the spindled balcony.

Detail of Bullfinch Pulpit

Newbury, N. H.

Charles Bullfinch is credited with adding beauty and design to the Colonial churches. He practiced architecture in the latter part of the nineteenth century.

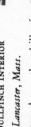

Back of the church building, of course, is the assumption that the individual soul is constantly engaged in a quest for God. The building should be an aid in that quest. That building is the best which gives the greatest aid to the worshiper as he seeks the Almighty. Since individual temperaments differ, one person may find the approach in the simple meetinghouse of the Society of Friends; the next may need the mighty cathedral with its strong walls and religious symbolism, one worshiper finds fully attended churches a stimulant to worship, while others prefer small, quiet altars; one needs the music of stately and majestic organs, while others will listen for the still small voice. It is difficult to define for one age, let alone seek to lay a foundation for those to come. Just what does constitute an adequate house of worship?

The wise leader will of course seek to find the lessons of history. During the years of Christendom what kinds of buildings have people in the past found best for the approach to God? There is no authorized type of architecture. Rather there has been a development from the early years. No committee ever sat down and decreed that the church should be built on a foundation laid in the form of a cross, or have a center pulpit, or a divided chancel. Instead adaptation to needs shaped the churches through the ages and produced the various historic types.

It might be well to glance for a moment at a brief survey of church architecture across the ages.

1. *Apostolic Churches.*—The first-century churches met in the homes of their wealthier members.

2. *The Basilican Church* (325-525).—At this early date

the churches had definitely adopted a type of architecture based on the Roman public building known as the basilica. The buildings were oblong with a narthex (foyer) at one end and an apse (a semicircular projection) at the other. This apse was used for seating the preachers and church dignitaries. Rome had found this type of building splendid for oratory. It was a period of great Christian preaching. Rows of columns divided the space into aisles. Extant examples of the basilican architecture include Santa Maria Magiorre and St. Paul's beyond the walls of Rome.

3. *Byzantine* (525-1453).—This is the name given to the architecture developed in Eastern Europe. The dominating exterior feature is the dome placed over squares by means of pendentives (vaulting).

4. *Romanesque* (775-1200).—The Romanesque is an introductory type. It is characterized by vaulted basilica, massive stone construction, and round arched openings. There is some experimentation with vaulting approaching true Gothic. In England, Durham Cathedral; in France, Saint-Martin, Tours; in Germany, Worms Cathedral; in Spain, Santiago de Compostela; in Italy, Milan Cathedral come from this period.

5. *True Gothic* (1160-1530).—This is the great age of church architecture. As Ralph Adams Cram says, "St. Peter's in Rome, though not a diocesan cathedral, and St. Paul's in London are not the structures we turn to for the most perfect embodiment of the idea of the Church in its glory, but rather Chartres and Amiens, Seville and Bourges, Durham and York and Gloucester and Lincoln." [2]

[2] *Church Building* (Boston: Marshall Jones Co., 1924), p. 174.

82

6. *Renaissance* (1420-1600).—This period of architecture in Europe was characterized by decorative richness and variety of form rather than a change in structural basis. Its greatest effect was seen in Italy and Spain where individual artists such as Alberti, Michelangelo, and Palladio influenced types of style. St. Peter's, Rome, comes from this period.

7. *Colonial* (1700 ——).—In America the name "Colonial architecture" is applied to the buildings constructed in the Colonies which reflect the contemporary work of the mother country. Early church buildings in the Southwest probably are Colonial structures in this respect. But use has limited the term to the style of the New Englanders. The early buildings were of wood. They were elegant, precise, yet dry in style, with a leaning toward classicism. The influence of Christopher Wren is seen in the steeples and spires. The use of decorative columns was quite common. This type of architecture, under the influence of Thomas Jefferson, influenced public life, and many of the plantation homes of the South followed the style. In many sections brick replaced the wood used in New England.

For the first time since the Colonial days America seems to be creating new styles of church architecture. There is a definite departure from the designing of the past. The Gothic which predominated up to the war days is definitely threatened. Out of this there may come an architecture which expresses the courage of American history and the pragmatic spirit of our day. We can look for interesting developments in church design.

A BYZANTINE INTERIOR

St. Bartholomew's Church, New York City

THE REVIVAL OF THE GOTHIC

The late Ralph Adams Cram probably did more than any other man to popularize the Gothic. His comments upon it may be taken as authoritative. He insisted that the English Gothic is the noblest expression of worship but cautions that the first years of the American revival of the Gothic were characterized by hard rules of imitation rather than creative planning. He says:

It knew little about the underlying principles, it was innocent of the old spirit, it could not, under industrialism, recover anything of the Mediaeval craft, it could not even copy intelligently, still it made shift to do with a sort of architectural shorthand and it faithfully tried to suggest what it could by no means accomplish.[8]

Mr. Cram believed that church architecture should have four qualities.

First, it is to be the house of God, the place of his earthly habitation. When a building aspires to this, it means that the worshipers will put into that holy place wealth and reverence.

In the second place, the church is to be a house set apart, where the mysteries of the Christian faith are to be solemnized. This means that the building will be built around the altar. The sacramental nature of the church stands second only to its recognition as the earthly habitation of the living God.

In the third place, the church must create the spiritual emotion through the ministry of all possible beauty of environment. Mr. Cram adds, and I think some readers will here disagree:

[8] *Ibid.*, p. 322.

Not in the barren and ugly meeting-house of the Puritans, with its whitewashed walls, three-decker pulpit and box pews, were men most easily lifted out of themselves into spiritual communion with God,—not there did they come most clearly to know the charity and sweetness of Christianity and the exalting solemnity of divine worship, but where they were surrounded by the dim shadows of mysterious aisles, where lofty piers of stone softened high overhead into sweeping arches and shadowy vaults, where golden light struck down through storied windows, painted with the benignant faces of saints and angels; where the eye rested at every turn on a painted and carven Bible, manifesting itself through the senses to the imagination; where every wall, every foot of floor, bore its silent memorial to the dead, its thank-offering to God; where was always the faint odor of old incense, the still atmosphere of prayer and praise.[4]

The fourth aspect of church architecture, to this great architect, is a building arrangement where the congregation may listen to the instruction of their spiritual leaders. It is natural to expect the architect to place the sermon fourth in his schedule of evaluation. In most of our Protestant buildings it has been placed first, and many times the first three principles have been entirely ignored. The designs of churches have been based on the desires of those who have made them possible. In an age which has made preaching the first and many times the only function of the church it is natural to expect buildings made for hearers. The corner pulpit with the fan arrangement of pews is the child of American revivalistic oratory.

Our Protestant churches are not willing to yield the

[4] *Ibid.*, p. 8.

86

primacy of the preaching mission, but, as this author understands it, they are ready to accept the first three principles.
Preaching will always have a most important place in the
program of our Protestant groups, and it must be recognized
in the architecture of the building. Extremists on both sides
have erred. The attention of one architect was called to the
fact that the church of his construction had several dead
sound centers of some proportion. He replied "That's not
important." But it is important. On the other hand the com-
plaint of a church trustee that several pews in the Gothic
structure were behind columns which shut off the view of the
pulpit hardly needs comment.

While Gothicism has had a strong emphasis in the new
American development, simple honesty makes us admit that
it is not the only historic type. Canon Streeter insisted that
the Gothic was a period type of architecture. In commenting
upon churches he said:

The most splendid Gothic cathedrals were, also, for those who
built them the best they could give, for their homes, also, were
Gothic—dark, cold, ill-aired but of their type beautiful.[5]

To this he adds:

Imitation Gothic in the midst of the ugly box-like tenements of
the poor is ugly and uncomely. What could be the best church
edifice that modern wealth in centers of civilization could produce?
We cannot tell, and never shall be able to tell until we get the beauty
of holiness in our homes, and return to simplicity and homeliness
in our churches.[6]

[5] B. H. Streeter *The Spirit* (New York: The Macmillan Company, 1935), p. 271.
[6] *Ibid.*

The homeliness suggested by Canon Streeter is making its appearance in some of the newer designs. They are much lower, lack the severity of line, but extend a friendly invitation. Unquestionably the Gothic will have more competition in the years ahead.

THE CHANCEL

The altar or Communion table is the center of worship in the church. The divided chancel which is so popular today is usually associated with Gothic architecture, but its installation does not designate a church as Gothic. Indeed, it has supplanted the center pulpit in many churches which have fairly pure Colonial lines.

Historically the Communion table has priority over the altar. It was the center of worship in the earliest church. It antedates the altar and also the pulpit. The spirit of the Communion table is that of the Lord's Supper; the altar has its origin in the catacombs of Rome, where the tomb of the deceased was used as the table. As the mass developed from the simple ceremony of the Lord's Supper, the altar came into its own. Its position at the east end of the chancel is impressive from the point of view of worship. So much has the position sold itself that some churches which will not yield to the altar use the divided chancel with the Communion table at the east end of the chancel. However, there is space back of it for the presiding minister. Traditions have developed around the use of the altar which define its shape, furnishings, and care.[7]

[7] A more extended discussion of this will be found in *The Altar in Your Church* by William H. Leach (New York: Goodenough & Woglom Co.).

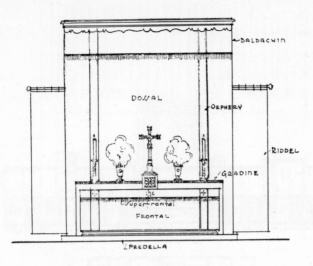

labels on figure:
BALDACHIN
DOSSAL
ORPHERY
RIDDEL
GRADINE
Supeafrontal
FRONTAL
PREDELLA

A CORRECTLY APPOINTED
ALTAR

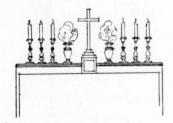

ARRANGEMENT WITH
SIX CANDLESTICKS

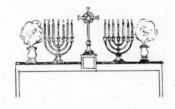

ARRANGEMENT WITH
SEVEN BRANCHED CANDLESTICKS
FOR FESTIVALS

ARRANGEMENT OF ALTAR APPOINTMENTS

Drawings by Bruce C. Wenner

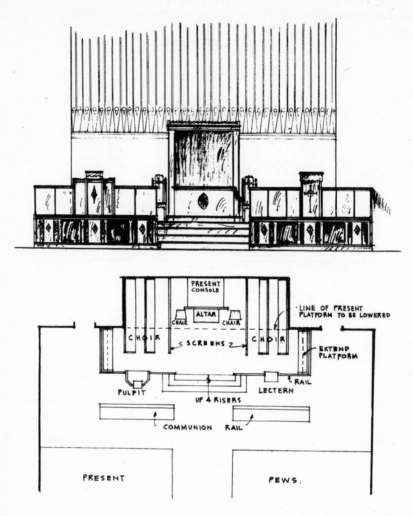

A REMODELED CHANCEL

Methodist Church, Danvers, Mass.

Illustration of architect's drawings for a new chancel. Note the problem presented by visible pipes of the organ. Pipes are still visible in this plan, but the console is back of the reredos.

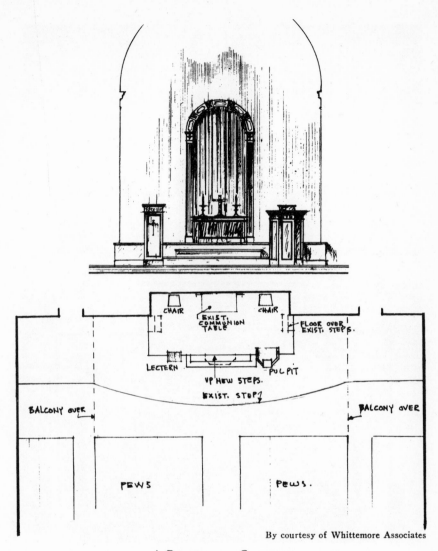

By courtesy of Whittemore Associates

A REMODELED CHANCEL

Pilgrim Congregational Church, New Haven, Conn.

Architect's plans for remodeling to provide a new chancel for the church. It was not necessary to provide for choir or organ in the chancel.

COMMUNION TABLE IN DIVIDED CHANCEL
Central Baptist Church, Norwich, Conn.

This church follows the severity of New England but has a divided
chancel. A Communion table, on which there are an open Bible and
two candlesticks, occupies the focal center of worship.

COMMUNION TABLE IN DIVIDED CHANCEL

Memorial Presbyterian Church, Grosse Pointe Farms, Mich.

The divided chancel is characteristic of the Gothic style of this church, which, however, follows Presbyterian custom in having a Communion table rather than an altar as the worship center.

To understand the divided chancel and its appointments keep in mind that the traditional church lies east and west and these terms are used conventionally even of churches facing other directions. The long rectangular section where the worshipers are accommodated in pews or chairs is known as the nave. At the other—the east—end. raised above the nave by one or more steps, is the chancel. Next to the nave is the choir; at the east end of the chancel is the sanctuary, where the altar is located. The sanctuary may be raised from the choir by other steps and separated by a railing which is the communicants' rail.

At the west end of the chancel nearest the worshipers are found the lectern, or reading desk, and the pulpit. The south side of the chancel is the epistle side, and for that reason some contend that the lectern should always be on the south side. The pulpit then stands at the other side, which is known as the gospel side. However, there seems to be little uniformity in this matter; the positions vary in different churches. Many churches also provide a prayer desk at a point conveniently near the minister's seat.

The choir may be separated from the nave not alone by the higher elevation but, many times, by an ornamental screen. This front of the chancel is known as the "choir" whether or not the church choir is seated there, but in the larger churches of correct design the choir does occupy this section, sitting in seats arranged on the north and south sides so that the members face the center.

Many Protestant churches do not have an altar at all and do not see the need of it. In a liturgical church where

94

COLONIAL WITH DIVIDED CHANCEL

First Methodist Church, Red Bank, N. J.

The window back of the altar has draw curtains to shut out light when necessary. Lantern fixtures, as recommended in Chapter XI, light the nave.

A DIFFERENT CHANCEL ARRANGEMENT

Messiah Lutheran Church, Philadelphia, Penn.

For the morning service this church has a divided chancel. The choir, seated parallel to the walls, is back of screens. For the evening service curtains are drawn to hide the altar. There is a center pulpit; and the choir, back of the minister, faces the congregation.

REVOLVING LECTERN

Epiphany Episcopal Church
Winchester, Mass.

Revolving lecterns are found
in many of the older churches.
It is difficult to find the origin
or the original use of the two
sides.

By courtesy of Whittemore Associates

Photograph by Simpson College Staff Photographer

OPEN BIBLE ON THE ALTAR

Chapel at Simpson College, Indianola, Ia.

The idea was planned and executed by students.

there is no altar, there is no church and no worship. The sanctuary is raised one step above the choir. Thus in the church there are three levels—the nave, the choir, and the sanctuary. The Roman Catholic rubric requires that the altar be made of stone. Protestant churches are more liberal in their interpretation, and their altars are of either stone or wood.

In the liturgical churches the altar is placed against the wall. Above it there may be a reredos (ornamental screen or wall back of altar) or appropriate dossal cloth (ornamental curtain for wall back of altar). Above the reredos windows are usually seen. The permanent "ornaments" of the altar are a cross or crucifix, two candlesticks with candles, a book desk known as missal stand, and a linen cloth. When the scene of the crucifixion or the figure of the cross is put into the reredos or dossal cloth, the cross is many times omitted from the altar itself. Some of the manuals which deal with the decorations of the altar go into detail on the size and purpose of the cloths or the altar.[8] The close detail does not concern us in this study.

There are some churches, usually those of the Presbyterian heritage, which build the divided chancel but keep the Communion table. It is placed in the position of the altar with the exception that there is space between it and the reredos for the minister to stand. The Communion is administered from back of the altar with the minister facing the congregation. A visitor to one of these churches sees, to all appearances, an altar, until the minister takes his place back of it.

Carl F. Weidmann, *A Manual for Altar Guilds* (Ernst Kaufmann, Inc.).

97

The baptismal font does not necessarily belong to the chancel. In early churches the baptistry was usually in a building apart from the church. Modern practice has moved it into the nave, and sometimes it is placed near the west end of the chancel. Correct practice would give it adequate housing at some convenient place near the west end of the nave. Of course in Baptist, Disciples of Christ, and other churches which practice immersion the font is replaced by a baptistry large enough for the rite of immersion. This is usually placed above or near the altar.

CHURCH FURNISHINGS

To produce a spirit of worship, there must be harmony in the furnishings of the church. Stained glass is almost as much a part of the building as is the pulpit. With the possible exception of the Colonial design, it is essential. Other furnishings, including the pews and lights, should be selected so that the whole may bring a spirit of unity to the worshiper. Clashes of types as well as colors are to be kept from the church.

Liturgists will insist that the floors be of stone. Not many churches of today follow the rule. But floors should be cushioned to eliminate as much noise as possible. If they are of wood, good carpeting placed over the wood will help. It is better than leaving hardwood flooring lightly finished, for it is then a source of noise and is usually slippery. There are various tile and composition floors which are satisfactory, but a good wooden floor covered with carpet usually meets

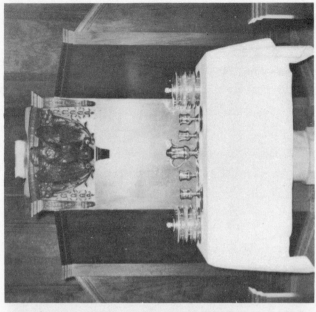

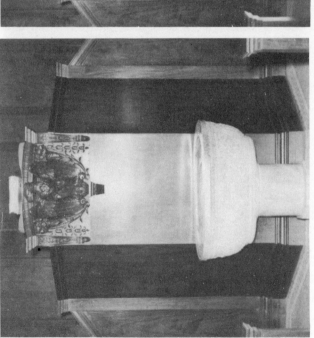

AN UNUSUAL BAPTISMAL FONT

Memorial Presbyterian Church, St. Augustine, Fla.

This marble baptismal font is directly under the center pulpit. It is converted into a Communion table for the observance of the Sacrament.

Designed by Whittemore Associates   Photograph by Bill Howard

BAPTISMAL FONT

Holy Trinity Episcopal Church, Tiverton, R. I.

The window above the font is covered in the summer months, which
adds a beauty to the plain design. Rail, candlesticks, and font are
hand-carved.

TILED BAPTISTRY

Broadway Baptist Church, Patterson, N. J.

Directly back of the altar in this church is the baptistry, lined with tile. Proximity to the altar brings together two great symbols of the Baptist heritage.

BEAUTY IN WOOD CARVINGS

Wood has a beauty all its own. *Above:* A hand-carved baptismal font
with a hinged cover. *Lower left:* A processional cross.
Lower right: A candlestick.

the requirements of a church. With modern vacuum cleaners, such a floor can be kept about as sanitary as any other type.

THE ORGAN

No one can discuss "Building for Worship" without having a few words to say about the organ. A good pipe organ is so closely related to the worship of God that with most fellowships it is an essential part of the church. The entire pipe organ craft has been developed around the church. Modern motion picture theaters rivaled the church for the interest of organ manufacturers for a few years, but sound pictures are driving the organ from the theaters, and again it has become an instrument of worship.

The development of radio amplification has made possible the so-called electronic organ. At first resisted by liturgists and organists, the electronic organ seems to have won a place for itself.

It is safe to make a general statement that no electronic organ has succeeded in producing, tone for tone, the quality of sound produced by a good pipe organ. At best it is a substitute. However, a good substitute is many times better than a poor pipe organ. Many small churches have taken advantage of bargains offered by theaters which have sought to get rid of their pipe organs. The results have not always been pleasing. A pipe organ is designed for the building where it will serve. An organ originally planned for a large structure but placed in a small auditorium is sure to prove offensive to sensitive ears. A good electronic organ is usually superior to a replaced pipe organ.

103

Pipe organ makers, in an effort to meet the competition of the electronic organs, have learned how to make good small organs. There are now several manufacturers who will provide pipe organs at a surprisingly low price. These organs are very effective. The small church should consider such organs when it is buying for worship. Visible pipes, once considered so important, are at present discouraged.

THE WINDOWS

Windows have traditionally made their contribution to the atmosphere of Christian worship. They have been used, not alone to let in the light, but primarily to symbolize the eternal truths of religion. Plain glass would of course admit more light than the close-leaded bits of colored glass. But the quest for worship has stimulated the making of windows of beauty and symbolism rather than windows to supply abundant light.

As John Donne said:

> Churches are best for prayer that have the least light,
> To see God, only, I go out of sight.

In the building of the New England churches the windows were made of transparent glass—at least as transparent as was available at the time. As in the other parts of the early American building native materials and economy played a most important part. Indeed where strict economy was necessary buildings were sometimes constructed with no windows. The Colonial style has continued in American churches, and the generally accepted windows for such architecture

104

Using Stained-Glass Windows in Remodeling

Presbyterian Church
Redwood Falls, Minn.

Above: What the minister faced, week after week, until the church was remodeled.

Below: The straight lines and the simplicity of the scene after the remodeling.

1   *3*   *4*

COSTS OF STAINED GLASS

Good stained-glass windows need not be expensive. Costs usually increase as details increase. In these examples the glass is all first class, the differences in cost lie in the details. The figures below may be used as a rough yardstick. There are, of course, other factors to be considered, such as distance from manufacturer, heighth of window from street level, and problems of installation. These figures, however, can be used quite generally.

Window 1—$ 7 per foot
Window 2—$10 per foot
Window 3—$15 per foot
Window 4—$20 per foot
Window 5—$35 per foot

2   *5*

By courtesy of Whittemore Associates

MEMORIAL WINDOW
Martin Luther Church (Lutheran), Cleveland, Ohio
A window which depicts the birth of Jesus, the crucifixion, the risen
Christ, and the Holy City is bordered with Bible symbols.

MEMORIAL WINDOW
First Baptist Church, Groton, Conn.
A recently dedicated window based on the Last Supper

are square or arch-topped, with small rectangular panes of glass. Recently many churches of Colonial design have installed stained glass. They have used retangular fenestrations to preserve the Colonial tradition, but have added to it the beauty of color and design. One outstanding example of this is the Church of the Abiding Presence at the Gettysburg Theological Seminary, Gettysburg, Pennsylvania. In churches of all other styles of architecture the accepted medium for windows is stained glass. The correct term is "stained glass" not "art glass." The accepted stained glass of today follows the best traditions of the past centuries. The large and somewhat gaudy picture windows of the last generation are giving way to those made of many small pieces of glass set in lead. Fine fenestration is most desirable. This, however, adds to the cost as well as the beauty. The cost of windows is based on the quality of the glass, the amount of work involved, and the size of the window.

The technique of making stained-glass windows has been borrowed from the fourteenth century. The delicate spots of color are not painted on the glass but are actually "pot" colors, so called because the glass is colored while in its molten state in the pot. The rendering of themes in glass is characteristic of the seventeenth and eighteenth centuries. The best practice in such work is to treat the subjects decoratively rather than realistically.

The most important windows in the church are those placed above the altar. One popular type for this purpose is the circular rose window. When the chancel is narrow and the ceiling high, three narrow lancet windows will perhaps

108

give better symmetry. It is well to point out that not all liturgists approve of a window above the altar. Such students point out that a beautiful window above the altar competes with it for attention. Thus it attacks the unity of worship.

In designing stained-glass windows for a church it would be well to start with the window above the altar and make that the center of any selected general motif. If money is not available for the installation of the most desirable windows, the church might install but one, or just a few, and then install others as funds are available. In the meantime cheaper temporary windows could fill the immediate needs. Even though the complete installation may be delayed for years, it is well to insist on good windows.

CHAPTER VII

Building for Christian Education

THE planning for an adequate building for Christian education must be based on two main objectives. First, the building and equipment should be planned to offer opportunities for the generally accepted phases of religious education. Second, provision should be made for division of the various age groups.

Christian education, as it is conceived today, does not consist merely of classrooms, lesson booklets, a teacher and pupils. Rather it seeks to utilize all approved procedures and materials which will enable the church school to aid in the Christian development of those who are enrolled in its classes.

What are some of the accepted ends of this education?

1. *Class Period.*—This is an intensive hour of religious training which is successfully accomplished only when the school has adequate teachers, competent lesson materials, and comparative isolation for the classes.

2. *Worship.*—Modern architecture for religious education is usually planned to provide departmental chapels where the pupils may worship through actual participation. The sanctuary of the church is made available for the adult groups. While the introduction of altars and symbols may help to

110

explain the theory of worship, it is becoming recognized that participation in worship, preferably conducted by a minister, is the best training in this field.

3. *Recreation and Social Expression.*—Fellowship is an essential part of Christian education, as it is a part of Christian society. Directed recreation and social activities give the church the opportunity to encourage the diffident, cheer the lonesome, and give right direction to the development of the aggressive. The value of social and recreational facilities in the educational building cannot be questioned. Planning the right type of rooms and materials will require wise judgment on the part of leaders.

4. *Visual Education.*—Very rapid strides are being made in all kinds of visual education. Projected pictures, both still and motion, are attaining increasing prominence. The installation of motion-picture projectors will require proper projection booths, security for the projectors, and other considerations. Supplementary needs will include a screen, electric power outlet, storage space, and similar items. Some churches may wish to set apart a special room for visual education. Even then it is probably wise to make plans for occasional showings in the departmental assemblies and individual classrooms.

5. *Dramatization and Pageantry.*—Drama has long been recognized as an aid of the church. Too often, however, it has been conceived as entertainment set up by the few for the many to witness. The best religious use of drama is to offer it as a program in which, under competent leadership, youth is taught not alone the techniques of production, but

111

Photograph by J. G. Allen & Son

CHURCH LIBRARY

Central Presbyterian Church, Lafayette, Ind.

This modern church library contains general and reference books. It has an endowment of five thousand dollars and has about fifteen hundred carefully selected volumes on the shelves.

A NURSERY

Sarah Hearn Memorial Church, Erie, Penn.

This is a good example of what a church can do to care for infants while parents are at worship. Walls and ceilings are high, with red trim. Varied colored crayon sketches of fanciful characters adorn the walls. Biblical verses, comprehensible to children, have been painted on the window sills.

also the moral and religious values of the plays which are dramatized. This means that the building should provide adequate stage, scenery, props, and facilities for costuming. Some suitable room in the church might be equipped with sewing machines for use in making the costumes. Such a room might well be combined with those which have been used in sewing for relief.

6. *The Library.*—The old-time Sunday school library was the forerunner of the modern public library. It offered fiction, biography, history, and religious books. In most communities there is little need for such libraries today. But every church of any size needs to make good books on religious education available to its leaders. Public libraries, as a rule, buy very few of the many good books on the subject. A central library in the church building, with good supervision, will be an asset. The individual classrooms might also have small shelves to contain some selected titles. Or the books might be placed on the teacher's table.

SUPPLEMENTARY NEEDS

While the above are primary recognized needs in an educational building, there are others which some churches are finding valuable.

1. *The Church Shop.*—The innovation of a woodworking shop in the church has proved a valuable medium in many communities. Under good leadership boys and girls learn the technique of making things with their hands. In some churches the men are the most eager to use the resources of

CHURCH WORKSHOPS

A well-equipped woodworking shop will make an attractive feature for your church. It can be used as an outlet for energy, for instruction in vacation school, and as a resource for voluntary production of many needed items and repairs in the church.

the shop. The result has been the construction of many useful items for the church.

2. *Hobby and Club Rooms.*—Churches may well encourage healthy hobbies whether they involve indoor or outdoor activities. Since there is always the danger of giving one small group too much importance in the church program, the leaders would do well to find out the various groups' hobbies and encourage the worth-while ones. Camera clubs are quite common in our churches. Skating, skiing, and hiking clubs have also been formed. Boy Scouts, Girl Scouts, and similar groups will need accommodations. Some of these may not require separate rooms, but it would be well to make some plans for facilities for them.

3. *Mothers' Room.*—This type of room has just recently come into the public eye. It consists of a soundproof room, located next to the sanctuary, where mothers with small children may sit. A soundproof glass partition separates the mothers and children from the worshipers, and a loudspeaker carries the sounds of the service into the room. If the room is in a balcony at the back, worshipers are in no wise disturbed.

4. *Sewing Room.*—The war years were crowded with church activities. Dining rooms and classrooms were turned into workrooms where women made bandages. Sewing machines were brought to the churches for their use. Many churches became conscious that those who had planned their church buildings had made no provision for this very necessary part of the modern church program.

As the list of special projects increases, one may become bewildered and wonder if every time one gets an idea it is going to be necessary to add a room to the church building. This will be discussed a little later in the chapter, but, to ease the mind of the reader, the list which has just been given is to show the breadth of the architectural needs. Most rooms, even the individual classrooms, will be utilized many times in the program of the church. Better facilities will be available if the committee which plans the building keeps the various objectives in mind.

BUILDING FOR AGE GROUPS

The church school usually is divided into departments. The departments in turn may be grouped by divisions. The educational building in the larger schools probably will be designed so that the department is the basis of the architectural unit; in the small schools the division will be the unit.

The grouping under the latter plan will be as follows:

1. Children's Division: the nursery, beginners, primary, and junior departments.
2. Young People's Division: the intermediate, senior, and young people's departments.
3. Adult Division: the young adults and adult Bible classes.

A building unit will consist of an assembly room and individual classrooms. In the larger schools the unit will be the department; in the smaller schools, if a department has but twenty to thirty pupils, the unit will be the division. A typical departmental unit is shown on the opposite page.

Each unit should be more or less self-contained. The assembly room may be a chapel; it probably should be if it is

116

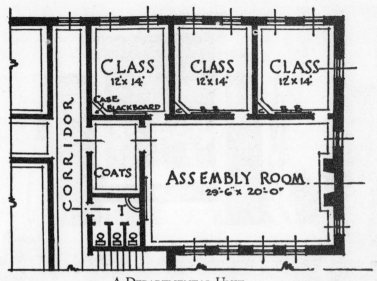

A Departmental Unit

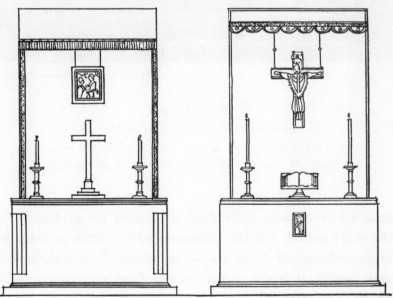

From drawing by Bruce C. Wenner

Class or Departmental Worship Centers

A SIDE CHAPEL

Grace Congregational Church, Framingham, Mass.
This chapel for all ages is furnished like the main
part of the church, to which it is connected.

used for devotions. Individual classrooms are preferred for
the study period. The best individual classroom is permanent-
ly partitioned off from the other rooms. It is well lighted
and heated. It has a carpet on the floor and strong, solid
chairs. The teacher has a table or desk. Wraps should have a
place near the assembly room so that it is not necessary for the

A CHILDREN'S CHAPEL

Arlington Street Church, Boston, Mass.

In this rather severe design, furniture has been cut to the size of the worshipers, and the chapel is connected to the church by a side door.

Photograph from Tile Council of America

A TILED CHAPEL

Bethlehem Chapel, Hansen Place Central Methodist Church, Brooklyn, N. Y.

Tile is used in this chapel both for floor and wainscot. It is colorful and lends itself to symbolic design. *Above:* Notice the insert in the wall, with the signs of the zodiac. *Below:* The design worked into the tile reredos is the tree of life. On the floor in front of the altar is a kneeling stone, brought from Bethlehem.

A TILED CHAPEL

St. Thomas Episcopal Church, New York City

In keeping with the historic design of the
church, tile is used for floors and aisles.

FLOOR SPACE NEEDED FOR STUDENTS

Groups	Ages for Each Department	Floor Space Recommended per Pupil in Attendance
Children's Division:		
Nursery (when small children attend)	Under 2½ or 3 yrs.	20-30 sq. ft. (not more than 10-12 children in 1 room)
Nursery Class	3 years	20-30 sq. ft. (not more than 15 children in 1 room)
Kindergarten or Beginners	4 and 5 years	18-25 sq. ft. (not more than 20-25 children in each room)
Primary	6, 7, and 8 yrs.	Workrooms for interest grades or classes, one of which will be large enough to seat all the children, 6-7 sq. ft. for each attendant. Class- and workrooms 15-18 sq. ft. for each.
Junior	9, 10, and 11 yrs.	6-8 sq. ft. in assembly room. Classroom 15-18 sq. ft.
Young People's Div.:		
Intermediate or Junior High	12, 13, 14 yrs.	8 sq. ft. in assembly room. Classrooms 12-18 sq. ft.
Senior	15-17 years	6-8 sq. ft. in assembly room; 8-15 sq. ft. in classrooms.
Young People	18-23 years	Same as for Seniors.
Adult Division:	24 and above	8-10 sq. ft. for classroom. Assembly usually taken care of in adult church worship or otherwise. Informal group procedure requires more space than usually provided in Adult Division.

Adapted from *Building and Equipment for Religious Education*, published by the Interdenominational Bureau of Architecture. Used by permission. It should be borne in mind that space requirements are not static. This table is but suggestive.

pupils to bring them into the classrooms. The rooms for the nursery, beginners, and primary groups should have tables and other essential equipment.

The departmental assemblies should be attractive and well lighted and heated. Closet and toilet facilities should be conveniently near. If the assembly room has not been built for a chapel, it should have some worship symbolism to give the impression of worship. An altar with candles, and with a dossal cloth hanging above it, will do much to encourage the spirit of devotion.

While the present-day tendency has been toward individual classrooms, some churches have carried the matter to a ridiculous extreme by creating for classes a series of small cubbyholes which are hardly inducive to study. Small churches combine their groups and thus plan for larger and more attractive rooms by treating an entire department as a unit, with boys and girls in the same class. This latter practice is an approved procedure which follows the lessons of the public schools.

It is also well to keep in mind that there will be a coupling of purposes with some of the rooms. Rooms used by classes on Sunday may be committee or social rooms on other occasions. The church may have one small chapel, which must be shared by the various divisions. This can be made satisfactory by having scheduling worship periods for the various divisions at different hours. A young people's group may use the same room on Sunday night that the women's class used in the day session. A choir assembly room may be made

Photographs by Dueringer Studio

A Young People's Room
First Methodist Church
Elgin, Illinois

A shoulder-high partition separates this room into two parts. One is the worship center, where services of devotion are held. The other is a social room that has a friendly fireplace.

available for a class meeting at an hour when it is not being used by the singers.

EQUIPMENT

Almost as essential as the room is the equipment which goes into it. Good chairs and tables should be provided. Well-built, strong chairs of the proper height for those using them should be carefully selected. Folding chairs, which usually twist and creak, are undesirable. The nursery will need sand boxes, toys, and pictures. The primary and possibly the junior department will want tables around which the children can gather. Chairs with desk arms for writing are worth while in all rooms. Such chairs encourage the pupil to take notes. Good Bible maps and a blackboard are essentials in youth and adult classrooms.

PICTURES

Suitable pictures should be selected for the walls of the various departments. Art should be good rather than profuse. If the child carries away the impression of one good picture from each department in which he has studied, the effort will be worth while. Among pictures which have been recommended for the various departments are:

For beginner's rooms: Hoppner, "The Sackville Children" (over mantel) ; Reynolds, "The Age of Innocence"; Miereveld, "A Child with a Parrot"; Reynolds, "Lady Gertrude Fitzpatrick"; Fragonard, "The Fair-haired Child"; Suardi, "Putto Under a Vine."

For primary rooms: Corregio, "Virgin and Child," detail from "The Holy Night" (over mantel) ; Cima da Conegliano,

125

PADDED DOORS ENHANCE AN ENTRANCE

St. Mary's Church, Akron, Ohio

The padded doors at the entrance to the nave add beauty. Note the brass studs in effective patterns. The material used in this instance is "Velon," a postwar plastic product.

"The Presentation in the Temple"; Cranach, "The Repose on the Flight into Egypt"; Dürer, "The Adoration of the Magi"; Raphael, "Saint George"; Fra Filippo Lippi, "An Angel Adoring."

For junior rooms: Fra Angelico, "The Annunciation" (over mantel); Pinturicchio, "A Young Knight Kneeling"; Giotto, "Saint Francis Preaching to the Birds"; Da Vinci, "Two Angels," detail from Verrocchio's "Baptism"; Fra Filippo Lippi, "The Holy Family"; Reynolds, "The Holy Family."

For intermediate rooms: Titian, "Madonna of the Cherries" (over mantel); Ford Madox Brown, "Christ Washing the Feet of Peter;" Gilbert Stuart, "George Washington."

For senior rooms: Raphael, "Madonna and Child," detail from the "Sistine Madonna" (over mantel); Raphael, "Madonna della Sedia" (alternate for over mantel); Rembrandt, "A Young Warrior"; Hoppner, "The Sisters"; Raeburn, "Boy with a Rabbit"; Sallman, "Head of Christ."

For young people's rooms: Da Vinci, "The Last Supper" (over mantel); Titian, "The Tribute Money"; Millet, "The Angelus"; Whistler, "Portrait of the Artist's Mother"; Da Vinci (attributed to), "Study for Head of Christ"; Rembrandt, "Holy Family."

For adult rooms, clubrooms, and parlors: Hobbema, "The Avenue" (over mantel); Rembrandt, "The Stone Bridge;" Claude Gellée, "Rest on the Flight into Egypt"; Corot, "Wood Gatherers"; Constable, "The Cornfield"; Cappelle, "A Calm."

CHAPTER VIII

Building for Fellowship

A church should be a brotherhood. The early churches met around supper tables, and the spirit of informality prevailed. When the church membership runs into the hundreds, it is not always simple to maintain the spirit of fellowship. In planning a new church it is wise to dedicate a substantial portion of the building to that end.

The dining room is a social "must" in any church building. Even the small pioneer church found an opportunity to gather its families for occasional church meals. Much has been said in ridicule of the church "social," but one cannot laugh off its social values. At times it may have savored of commercialism, but the few dollars the good ladies made for the church was the smaller asset. The greater was the opportunity offered for friendly get-togethers.

The social program of the modern church will not, however, end with the meals. The same hall in which the meals are served must serve other ends. It will probably be used also as a game room. It will serve as a theater for dramatic productions. It will accommodate meetings which are so purely secular that it is not wise to hold them in the sanctuary. It will be a social gathering place for youth and family groups. Its floor may be used for handball, volleyball, and shuffleboard.

In planning the room all of the anticipated activities should be kept in mind. Should the ceiling be too low, certain games are eliminated. If no stage is constructed, dramatics are out. If the floor is not satisfactory, folk dances are impracticable. If it is not easily accessible, visitors will be discouraged.

Because it must be a large room, the space directly under the sanctuary seems the natural one to most people. However, the extra excavation necessary may offset any savings natural to such a location. When there is space available above the ground, light, heat, and air requirements favor the latter position.

The fellowship hall should have a good floor. Many types of wooden and composition floors are now available. The tables and chairs should be of substantial construction. There are some strong folding chairs available. If folding chairs are necessary, and they do seem to be at times, they should be of sufficient strength to stand firmly while occupied. They should be comfortable. There is nothing so disconcerting to the person listening to a discussion or eating at a table than to sit in a chair which wobbles. One instinctively braces himself to escape injury and is not able to relax and get the most from the occasion.

Tables, also, should be strong enough to bear the weight of dishes, food, and elbows. These tables cannot remain standing all of the time. They must have some kind of collapsible feature. If one has observed the tables available for special banquets at hotels, he has learned this lesson. The tables are put in position and removed easily, yet they have sufficient strength. A popular table for hotels has a circular top and is large enough to seat eight people. The detachable legs are strongly made and fold into a flat position. With the circular tops serving as wheels, the tables are easily rolled into storage when they are no longer needed.

The logical storage space for the church dining-room furniture is under the platform, where there is one. In this case we will assume that the room is going to be used for public gatherings and dramatics. If so, a stage is necessary, and the space under the stage is valuable for this storage. When rectangular tables are used, some churches have solved the problem of mobility by having a low truck, known as a "dolly," for use in moving this furniture about. These trucks often have four-inch rubber-tired, ball-bearing wheels. This increases their mobility and practicability.

A dining room would be a poor place without an adjacent and adequate kitchen. Church meals are usually prepared by voluntary workers, and the need for ample space is thus imperative, though even skilled kitchen help must have room in which to move.

The kitchen should be equipped with good labor-saving helps, such as a large range, an iceless refrigerator, a large sink, cabinets for dishes, and counter space—where nothing else is against the wall. The best place for a steam table is in the center of the kitchen. The servers then can work from both sides of the table.

There should be double doors with kick plates, one for entrance and one for exit. These doors should be clearly marked, so that no one will take the wrong way and thus cause confusion and wreckage. Dining-room waitresses should

Photograph by Zito Studios

A Model Church Kitchen
Broadway Baptist Church, Patterson, N. J.
Critics have called this kitchen a model of efficiency.
It was designed by a prominent restaurant man.

not enter the kitchen. A serving counter between the two rooms will make it possible for the kitchen servers to put the filled dishes on the counter for the table waitresses. A good place for the coffee urn is at one side of this serving table. The counter is also very convenient when buffet service replaces table service. Cafeteria-style meals are easily arranged with this equipment.

Some churches do not like to have the serving counter set in the wall between the dining room and kitchen. They pre-

131

fer to build a serving room, which is located between the kitchen and the dining room. Kitchen workers place the food on tables in this room. The servers do not go into the kitchen. Double doors will make it possible to enter this room at one side, pick up the dishes, and leave by the other side.

Many of the newer labor-saving devices are making their way into the church kitchen—electric dish-washing machines, electric potato peelers, bread-slicing and meat-slicing machines, and other aids to efficiency which increase the opportunities or time for fellowship.

KITCHENETTES

Churches of any size will want to provide additional kitchen and dining-room facilities by installing kitchenettes. There are many social meetings where the small kitchen serves better than the larger one. A youth class wants a spread after one of the meetings. The women's meeting in the afternoon may be followed by a "spot" of tea. A small kitchen may be used many times to an advantage, thus saving light and heat. Several luncheon meetings may be held in the church at the same time. Kitchenettes will be an essential in the church of the future.

FELLOWSHIP USES OF THE DINING ROOM

The dining room will probably also be used for fellowship in many other ways. It can be a game room. If the ceiling is high enough, the tables can be stored away for basketball and volleyball. If the ceiling is too low for these games, a few shuffleboard courts can be made. Large gatherings of children

132

will have their games in this room. If the church encourages social dancing, this will be the logical room for the larger get-togethers. It will be the one room in the church where family nights will be possible.

DRAMATIC PRODUCTIONS

The stage in this room should be adequate for dramatic productions, but the size of the stage is not the only problem. On either side there is need for dressing rooms and storage. The wall of the building should not be the back of the stage. Instead, a drop or partition is necessary to furnish passageway. A fireproof curtain at the front of the stage is essential. The old formal rolling drops are not necessary today. They have been replaced by more flexible drapes which have both beauty and utility. Lighting effects, including footlights, are a necessary part of the equipment. The well for the footlights can have a cover, which hides them when the stage is used for lectures and meetings.

Some of the simple rules to be followed in designing the stage are:

1. The stage should not be too high. Three to four feet is correct.
2. Hardwood should never be used for stage floors. Use a soft wood in which nails may be driven without splitting the lumber.
3. The best scenery is suggestive rather than realistic.
4. Lighting is the most vital part of the stage equipment. It highlights the actors; it suggests the hour of the day and even the seasons of the year.

Religious drama has become such an important part of the modern church school curriculum that the building committee should carefully consider providing stage room and other facilities for the proper presentation.

CHURCH PARLORS

There is need in churches of any size for church parlors, which are really parlors in that they provide the comfort and utility of the living-rooms of our homes. They offer the opportunity for rest with fellowship. They are the logical place for meetings of the women's Bible class. Joint committees of any size will find the parlors a good meeting place. The parlors should not be allowed to become dingy or barren. A carpet should be on the floor and good pictures on the wall. The furniture should appeal to the aesthetic sense.

Perhaps when a parlor is prepared for youth or men, it should be called the "lounge," as some churches so name it. An interesting combination room in the First Methodist Church, Elgin, Illinois, provides a lounge and worship center. The lounge end of the room is separated from the chapel by a shoulder-high partition. The center of attraction in the lounge is the open fireplace. The room is friendly and inviting.

The Methodist Church of Leonardsville, New York, was built at a time when a large auditorium dominated the entire structure. In remodeling to provide social and educational facilities it was found possible to reduce the size of the auditorium and to place a ladies' parlor at the rear. This was separated from the sanctuary by a partition with folding windows. When there are overflow congregations, opening the windows makes the parlor essentially a part of the sanctu-

134

ary. This plan is available for many churches which plan to remodel their buildings.

The First Church of the Brethren, Cleveland, Ohio, uses its ladies' parlor as a mother's room. This is a balcony room, which has been prepared over the foyer next to the sanctuary. A glass partition, which consists of two large sheets of glass with air space between them, is the partition that separates the parlor from the sanctuary. The room is sound proof. Loudspeakers bring the message of the minister and the music. In this parlor ladies with children may gather during the service. The children may amuse themselves with toys without disturbing the congregation. The mothers have oversight of their children and, at the same time, have the advantage of seeing, hearing, and participating in the worship services.

AUXILIARY FEATURES

Bowling alleys are important in the program of many churches. Bowling is a clean recreation, and very seldom does one hear any criticism of its use. Bowling alleys, however, are expensive and require considerable space. Two alleys must have a width of eleven and one-half feet. Each alley must be eighty-three feet in length. If a gallery for spectators is to be made available in the rear, there must be additional space allowed when planning the length of the room.

If more strenuous sports such as handball or volleyball are held in the fellowship halls, shower facilities should be installed.

Some churches have installed swimming pools. Such pools

are expensive to construct, expensive to maintain, and are probably the least necessary of the auxiliary features.

A projection booth for the fellowship hall is desirable if motion pictures are to be shown. The usual rule is to place the booth at the rear of the room if there is no balcony; if the room has a balcony, place the booth at the front of the balcony. The purpose of the booth is to provide safety, to make the proper electrical outlets available, and to give the operator sufficient room for his purpose.

The church is fortunate if it has sufficient real estate for out-of-door meeting places for classes. Small groups, during the warm months, will appreciate such meeting places if they are screened by bushes, hedges, or trees. Church gardens are interesting and effective places of fellowship. An open-air fireplace where picnics may be held can become a most valuable asset to a church.

CHAPTER IX

Building for Administration

JUDGING from the available literature on church architecture, this is the neglected area in church building. The need for adequate facilities where the detailed administrative work of the church can be conducted effectively seems to be a mystery to most people. Some churches which have been built in the last twenty-five years have failed almost entirely to provide such facilities. Other rooms, not at all suitable, have been converted into use for the purpose.

The average church needs an office in which the pastoral affairs of the parish may center; a room where the church school secretaries may conduct their work and keep their records; a meeting place for church boards where necessary administrative data will be accessible. The space necessary will be determined largely by the membership of the church and by the paid and voluntary personnel involved.

The first step in the establishment of the church office is usually made by the minister, who sets up, in some convenient place, a combination study and office. One room suffices him for pastoral consultations, study hours, and business conferences, but we can still question the wisdom of this combination room. If there is space for the study in the parsonage, he will probably do better to have his study in his home. Then the single room in the church will be an office. He may set definite office hours. His study period is thus divorced from the executive procedures, which is wise. In answer to this many ministers will say that their hours in the single combination office room and study are undisturbed by callers. There is merit to both sides of this question.

Every church building should, if possible, provide an office in the church. If it is to offer facilities for study, it is well for the office to be divided into two parts. The visitor will enter a little reception room. It need not be large. Then there should be an inner room which will contain the minister's library and desk. Even if the minister does not have a secretary to welcome callers, it is a simple matter for him to step out to the reception room to greet visitors and to answer simple inquiries. Consultative cases will be taken into the study. The main idea is to have a partition which keeps the minister's inner sanctum separated from the details of calls and office routine. If a secretary is employed, she will work in the reception office. The dictation will probably be given in the study, but the typing will be done at the secretarial desk in the reception office. The telephone calls will be taken there, and the minister will have more time for his study.

The conflict of purposes between the office and the study is that, while any office should be accessible, a minister's study should be more or less isolated. The minister must be ever willing to meet those who seek his help. The latchstring should be out. But he himself must have some protection for study hours. Some people seeking pastoral help will hesitate to go to the parsonage; they will go to the church.

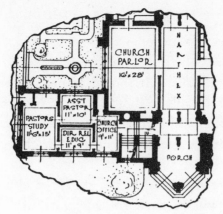

OFFICE PLANS

Wenner & Fink, Architects

Trinity Methodist Church, Albany, N. Y.

The plans show a good arrangement for the church with professional staff. The first entrance is to the office. The pastor's study is given protection beyond the office of his associates.

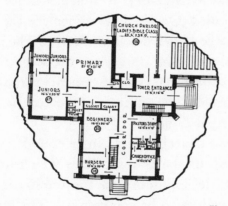

Glen H. Thomas, Architect

OFFICE PLANS

Grace Presbyterian Church, Wichita, Kan.

Note that the office is near an entrance and that the visitor will instinctively call at the office seeking the pastor's study. This gives the minister some security from visitors during study hours.

The architect should plan a new church so that the church office is located where it is easily accessible to mailmen, delivery men, and callers. It should be near an entrance which has a walk. Preferably it should have a sign which points the way to the office. It should never be necessary for one to walk through one of the assembly rooms of the church to get to the church office.

As members are added to the staff, the church offices will grow. There will be need for adequate files. Any associate minister will need his consultation room. The pastor's study can then be placed more in the background, and he will not have the confustion which confronts the minister who is forced to do double or triple duty. I have always thought that Westminster Presbyterian Church, Buffalo, New York, offers one of the most satisfactory arrangements for the offices. Two floors are used. On the lower floor are the accounting office and the office of the associate minister. The pastor of the church has his study and library on the second floor. He is accessible only as one makes arrangements through the office on the lower floor. The offices are located near the main entrance to the parish house.

It is well if the church offices can be considered as a unity, serving the needs of the church. Plans which have an office in one part of the building and the minister's study in a different part are not to be commended. The minister gains little additional privacy in such a plan and has counter annoyances to offset any gains. The offices should be planned as a unit and located near a main entrance. Being self-contained, they should have their own toilet facilities. If wash-

140

rooms and toilets have been installed conveniently near, this will be sufficient.

The specialization of tasks has caused some churches to provide the minister an additional room for counseling. In Trinity Methodist Church, Youngstown, Ohio, this room is distinct from the study and office. Furnishings were provided to create the proper atmosphere for pastoral conferences. The Court Street Methodist Church, Rockford, Illinois, has provided the consultation room in the church, but the minister's study has been moved to a commercial building.

RECORDS TO BE KEPT IN THE OFFICE

Only in a small church which has no employed clerical help will records ever be kept in individual homes. All valuable data, both parish and financial, should have a place of security in the church office. Offerings should be counted there. Membership cards should be kept there. A fireproof filing case or vault is necessary for the proper protection of the historic records and the currency, and in planning the office provision should be made for a place for this vault.

It is well if the room where trustees, stewards, elders, deacons, and others meet be near the church office so that access is had to data on file there. There is a wide variety of practice in the duties of a church secretary. But all will agree that one of her first duties is so to organize the files of the church that data necessary for the various meetings of the church are always available.

It must be remembered that a minister may keep personal records to supplement the official records of the church. The

141

A ROOM FOR COUNSELING

Trinity Methodist Church, Youngstown, Ohio

With the thought that counseling is quite apart from administration
and sermon preparation, this church has provided its minister with
a room for counseling.

church records are not his property. They belong to the
church. He has access to them as the minister. But for his
pastoral work he will have his own properly annotated calling
list and other records.

SUNDAY SCHOOL RECORDS

Any church being built today should have a room for the
officials of the church school and a depository for its records.
The secretarial work in the church school is usually on a

voluntary basis. There is much to be done in a single hour. Classbooks must be passed out, offerings taken and entered, class rolls checked, and attendance figures recorded. This can be done most effectively when a room is provided for the purpose. Sunday school records, like those of the church, are lost when carried from the building for keeping in a private home.

The ease of operation where a special room and equipment are provided the church school superintendent and secretary will pay for itself many times in efficiency.

CHAPTER X

Electronics and Amplification

M ANY churches today make use of electronic amplification of one form or another. Occasionally, we find a church which utilizes such aids to the utmost. They are of great value in the services of worship, in Christian education, in outdoor publicity, and in many other ways. So recently has the science of electronics been developed that few churches have been properly wired for its effective use. Wires are now strung over cornices and pictures and hidden behind moldings. It is not at all uncommon for unsightly black wires to be hung in plain sight in an otherwise perfectly appointed chancel.

The following list contains some of the many uses of electronic amplification. These uses are given in the order of their importance to the churches which have tried the devices.

1. *Pew Phones.*—For nearly a generation the churches have had the use of pew phones for the deaf. A few pews are set aside for the hard-of-hearing. A microphone on the pulpit carries the minister's voice through the wires to the receivers in these pews.

At first the phones were operated by batteries. As the strength waned, the efficiency lessened. Yet, in spite of their limitations, these phones carried the gospel message to many who would have been otherwise deprived of it.

144

Today's pew phones are connected to the building current. They are not disturbing to the congregation. Crystal receivers transmit the music and the spoken word without distortion to those who need this aid. The price of installation is but a fraction of the cost of the old-time battery-operated sets.

2. *Acoustical Correction.*—Poor acoustics have dimmed the force of much preaching, but may now be improved in many cases through the use of some of the modern plasters and wall-boards. Another method is the use of skillfully placed loud-speakers, which bring the voice, clear and strong, to all parts of the room. I use the word "skillfully" without reservation, for a poor installation will cause so much distortion that the congregation may question the merits of the use of the amplifying system. Churches should be warned that the installation of any system of electronics is a job for a skilled technician.

3. *Overflow Meetings.*—Once the speakers are installed, it is a simple matter to provide additional speakers for overflow meetings. For instance, Easter is almost sure to bring a more-than-capacity audience. The entire building may be filled, and extra speakers will be needed to carry the music and the sermon to these rooms.

Some variation of this is seen in plans for bringing the music and the sermon to the nursery, where mothers are with their children. In some churches the installation of a speaker in the choir assembly room has brought the strains of the organ, so that the singers may find it easy to start their processional hymn at the right moment.

4. *Portable Address Systems.*—Churches found out very early that open-air meetings can be better controlled through

145

the use of such systems. They have been carried to the park for Easter sunrise services and for evening vespers. The director of the Sunday school picnic knows the value of such a system.

5. *Record Players.*—Phonograph records are becoming more important to the church. Already many records are available for the teaching of missionary stories and Sunday school lessons. Small gatherings have provided music and evening addresses through the use of records. Played through the amplifying system, the message of a record may be carried to every room in the church.

If the church has a recording machine, services may be recorded and later played back for other gatherings, or even carried to the homes of the sick.

6. *Radio.*—There is a two-way use of radio in the church. First, there is the use of radio broadcasting. If a radio station is to pick up the minister's service or some other feature of a service, the church will need to have microphones set up at the proper places. There is also need for receiving sets. Audiences may wish to listen to messages being broadcast from conventions or other meetings. The church receiver will pick up the broadcast and transmit it over the public address system to the various parts of the church.

7. *Tower Music.*—This popular feature has found ready acceptance. It is of course a substitute for tower chimes. If the church organ is equipped with chimes, the amplifying system is used to broadcast the music from a speaker placed in the church tower. Where there are no organ chimes, small tubular chimes or a carillon can be installed for use in broad-

146

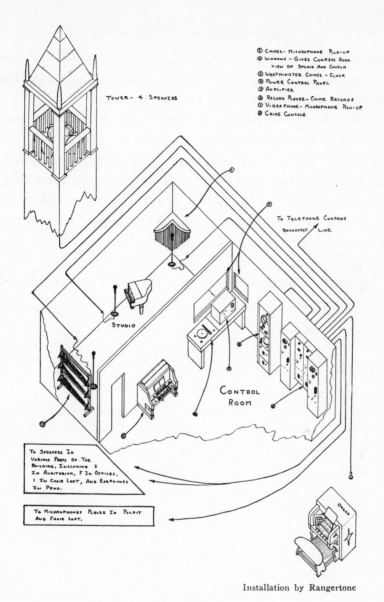

TOWER - 4 SPEAKERS

① CHIMES - MICROPHONE PICK-UP
② WINDOWS - GIVES CONTROL ROOM
   VIEW OF STUDIO AND CHURCH
③ WESTMINISTER CHIMES - CLOCK
④ POWER CONTROL PANEL
⑤ AMPLIFIER
⑥ RECORD PLAYER - CHIME RECORDS
⑦ VIBRAPHONE - MICROPHONE PICK-UP
⑧ CHIME CONSOLE

TO TELEPHONE COMPANY
BROADCAST LINE

STUDIO

CONTROL ROOM

TO SPEAKERS IN
VARIOUS PARTS OF THE
BUILDING, INCLUDING 2
IN AUDITORIUM, 5 IN OFFICES,
1 IN CHOIR LOFT, AND EARPHONES
IN PEWS.

TO MICROPHONES PLACED IN PULPIT
AND CHOIR LOFT.

ORGAN

Installation by Rangertone

THE AMPLIFICATION SYSTEM
First Methodist Church, Los Angeles, Calif.

casting through the tower amplifiers. Some churches which possess no chimes have used record players and good chime recordings for broadcasts from the tower.

The selection of proper equipment for the various types of electronic amplification may not be in the jurisdiction of the building committee. The architect and committee, however, should be aware of the value of amplification and should make provision for it by the installation of an adequately equipped control room. Small and compact control units are available. The control room need not be large, but a centrally controlled system is very desirable.

Electronic organs have been discussed in Chapter VI, "Building for Worship."

CHAPTER XI

Lighting

THE church building is the scene of varied activities, and the lighting must be adapted to the particular purposes to which each room is assigned. The nave and chancel require special consideration, as their uses are peculiar to the House of God. If traditional practice is followed—as seems to be wise—the church will not be too light. John Donne was probably right when he insisted that men see God best when the house of prayer is not too well lighted. Milton's "dim religious light" is necessary to put a congregation at ease. However, there is need of sufficient light to enable the congregation to follow the prayers and to read the hymns and responses.

The apparent conflict of these two aims has led to the practice of installing facilities for two kinds of lighting in the church. The first is the kind currently known as "general" lighting. This is a soft, somber light, which is diffused enough for worshipers to enter and leave the nave. It is not bright enough to distract from worship. Two foot-candles gives the illumination which is usually thought sufficient for this purpose. But, in addition to this light, there is need for "specific" lighting.

Four areas which need specific lighting are: (1) pew areas

149

(to permit easy reading of responses and hymns), (2) pulpit and lectern (to permit easy reading of the Scriptures and the manuscript of the sermon), (3) the choir (to enable the members to follow the words and music), and (4) the altar or sanctuary (the center of worship). The lighting of these four areas needs to be controlled so that it may be used only when necessary and will not become part of the generalized lighting.

The most practical type of general lighting, and probably the least expensive, is the lantern type of fixture. While a church may invest in such fixtures at a large cost, simple parchment lanterns, constructed for a few dollars each, will be just as attractive and satisfactory. The Cathedral of St. John the Divine in New York City has the best possible wiring. It is concealed in the masonry and will last for generations. But the lighting fixtures for nave and chancel consist of parchment cylinders, open at the top and bottom, each of which contains a frosted bulb of three hundred or two hundred watts capacity. This arrangement permits the chancel to have eight foot-candles, while at pew level the lighting is reduced to five foot-candles.

There is much that can be said for the lantern type of fixture. It diffuses the light horizontally through glass or parchment, which softens the brilliance. The design of the cylinders may be pleasing. The vertical walls of the lanterns catch much less dust than does the more ornamental type of fixture. Recent developments in lighting leave the bottom and top of the lantern open so that the specific lighting for pews may be obtained from this one fixture. In such lanterns

150

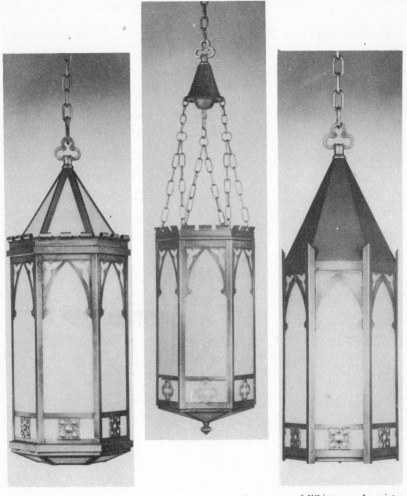

Church Lanterns

These lanterns are the type recommended
for general lighting of nave and chancel.

reflecting surfaces around the bulb emit the light downward through an aperture, whence it continues in a conical beam until it reaches the surface to be lighted. It should be said, however, that this combination of general and specific lighting is still largely in the experimental stage.

The more commonly practiced plan for adding the specific to the general lighting requires installation of concealed projectors to give the necessary foot-candle light on the object. A good example is the Riverside Church in New York, where the original lighting in the nave consisted of ten very fine chandeliers. These were satisfactory for the general lighting but at the pew level produced but one half foot-candle. Specific lighting was therefore installed for the pews. This consists of a set of projectors concealed in the vaulting. The projectors, of 1000-watt capacity, added about four foot-candles to the pew lighting. This gives sufficient illumination for reading.

Projectors properly placed will give the pulpit and lectern illumination. Such light should be projected at an angle of forty-five degrees, or steeper, so that the preacher will have light to read, and so that his face will be clearly visible to the congregation. While this light should be sufficient for these two purposes, it should not have the intensity of stage lighting in the theater. The function of the preacher is quite different from that of the actor. Some churches, in blind imitation of movie practices, darken the nave and throw an intense floodlight upon the minister. The nave of the church should never be so dark that the minister cannot see the faces of his congregation.

152

The same principle applies to the lighting for the choir. The altar need not be as brightly lighted as the pulpit and choir, but its lighting should be more constant. Usually the sanctuary and altar remain lighted during the entire service, and perhaps during all of the hours that the church is open to worshipers.

Each facility for specific lighting should have its own circuit and switch. A rheostat is usually desirable, so that the light can be dimmed or brightened, as well as cut off and on.

LIGHTING EDUCATIONAL AND SOCIAL ROOMS

The rules of lighting for the church nave do not, of course, apply to other parts of the church building. The lighting in the educational, social, and administration rooms will be like that adopted for schools and business offices. Little experimentation has been done in lighting rooms especially for religious education purposes.

The foot-candle power in these rooms must be many times more than that desirable at pew level in the nave. Study desks, office desks, and work tables need thirty to eighty foot-candles. Glare, of course, is undesirable. As in the case of nave lighting the cost of the fixtures is not indicative of their efficiency. In the smaller classrooms several indirect lighting fixtures, using incandescent bulbs, will be most effective. One very satisfactory fixture is based around a bulb that has a frosted bottom. The reflector which fits around this bulb reflects the light upward and out. This fixture costs much less than some of the heavy globe fixtures now used in churches and does a much better job of diffusing the light.

Photographs courtesy of Westinghouse Electric Corporation

OFFICE AND CLASSROOM LIGHTING

Little experimentation has been done in efficient lighting for church offices and educational rooms. The illustration above shows good lighting for a church office. Thirty to eighty foot-candles are needed. The indirect lighting recommended for public-school libraries comes close to meeting classroom needs. Light equal to that of the office is essential.

In the larger rooms and in the church office continuous indirect lighting is most effective. This type of fixture may use either incandescent or fluorescent bulbs. The luminaires are placed at high level around the desks so that there is no direct glare into the eyes.

CHAPTER XII

Heating, Cooling, and Air Conditioning

Heating, cooling, and air conditioning should be considered together because the units should be designed and engineered as one job, if a church is to have all three. Every church in the United States needs some kind of a heating system. Comparatively few churches, to date, have installed air conditioning. The same system which distributes heat can be utilized to distribute fresh, cooled air. The best time to make a decision on whether to have air conditioning is in the planning of the new building. Air conditioning has not seemed essential to many churches because they are closed for the warm months. If a church plans a year around program, it is quite possible that a good cooling system will help popularize the summer services. Such units have evidently been effective in motion-picture theaters.

HEATING

Every section of the United States has some cold months when heat is necessary in the church. The type of heating system used should depend upon the climate and the size of the building. Either a hot-air or a steam system with radiators is satisfactory for the small church. Since many times the caretaker is an amateur, it is best to have a simply designed heating unit. The fuel may be natural gas, oil, or coal. If coal is used,

156

the firing will be accomplished most efficiently by a stoker.

Hot-air heating is direct and simple. It is always desirable, though, to have cut-out dampers in the air ducts so that rooms in use may be heated without also heating the entire building. Air outlets in the nave and chancel should be installed in the window sills. Intake grills for the return of the cold air may be placed at the floor level. Forced circulation of air makes it possible to place the furnace at one end of the basement, with the air ducts between the floor joists so that they are not in the way.

When steam heat is used, the radiators in the nave should be placed under the windows, with the grills installed in the window sills. The addition of fans for redistribution of the hot air at strategic points will prove economical.

Radiators and recirculating units may also be used in the fellowship hall. If the hall is in the basement, manually operated air intakes will help give the necessary fresh air and ventilation.

Heating by radiation is being recommended for larger churches. This system, which may be comparatively new to the layman, is well known in the field of engineering. It is one of the most simple methods of heating, but the equipment for it must be installed at the time of building. This equipment consists of copper or wrought-iron pipes placed in the concrete or masonry floors. Warm or hot water flowing through these pipes warms the rooms and hence the air. The heat is controlled by the temperature of the water.

While all the systems mentioned here have been satisfactorily installed, many engineers recommend that floor radiation be used as the basic method of heating, and that it be supplemented by hot-air or steam radiators in special places. Floor radiation might be used as the main heating unit, and supplementary methods, with air circulation, could then be used for the additional heat desired.

In a church of any size it is necessary to zone the heating or to have individual radiator control. Zoning is the method through which one part of the church—the part in use—is kept at the desired temperature, while unused portions of the building are kept without heat. The following zones could be recommended: (1) the twenty-four-hour zone, consisting of the entrance halls, the chapel for private devotions, the church offices, the minister's study, and the toilets; (2) the fellowship hall, which includes the dining room and the kitchen; (3) the nave, chancel, and foyers; (4) classrooms; and so on. Some churches prefer automatic controls, operated by thermostats, on the radiators in the various rooms.

If steam is used for the supplementary heat or for the complete heating of the church, the radiators should be set under the windows with grills in the window sills. The additional circulating units should be installed for ventilation and for the greatest economy in operation. Since the nave of the church is usually high, the hot air has a tendency to go to the ceiling. Some method of circulation must be found to overcome this natural tendency. The chancel with a low ceiling needs its own air circulating unit for ventilation.

The furnace may be operated by natural gas, oil, or coal. The cost of each varies in different parts of the country. Natural gas is not available in all localities, so the real com-

INSTALLATION OF RADIANT HEATING

Trinity Evangelical Lutheran Church, Norfolk, Va.

Wrought iron pipes provide the grids for radiant heating. Four inches of concrete were laid over and around these pipes. This was covered with a tile floor.

petition is probably between the oil and coal industries. They compete in quality as well as price. Both are subject to strikes and delays in transportation. Perhaps the best policy for the church is to have two furnaces, one for oil and the other for coal. Oil furnaces are entirely automatic. If coal is used, a stoker should be installed for economy in heating costs.

COOLING

There are a number of methods of cooling the church for the summer months. Some of these ways are quite simple and inexpensive. For example, some years ago a Kansas City church, at the suggestion of the choir leader, loaded two tons of ice into its hot-air furnace. The fans were turned on and, instead of hot air, cooling air came out of the registers. A Long Island church which had a metal roof secured a fire hose and played cold water over the roof for an hour. The result was a cooler temperature in the church. The first of these methods proved very expensive; neither was efficient. But they do illustrate the principle of artificial cooling.

If the church has a low-pressure hot water heating system, the temperature of the building may be reduced by running cold water through the system. To be effective the water must have a temperature of less than 55 degrees. Once it becomes warm, it is ineffective. In most localities the water from the public utility is not cool enough and is too expensive for this use, so it is necessary to drill wells near or under the churches. Where water of the correct temperature is available an electric pump can be used to force it through the pipes of the heating system to cool the building. No church, however, should undertake to cool its building in this way without first consulting a heating engineer to make sure that its circulating system is adapted to this plan.

Because a church is used but a few hours a week, it requires less refrigeration than does a business building with the same number of cubic-feet of space. This fact has made it possible for churches to take advantage of a new development in air refrigeration. Instead of cooling the air continuously, the cooled water remains stored in a large bottle. On Sunday it is released for cooling the church. As a much smaller refrigeration unit is required than would be necessary if the water were used as cooled, the cost of refrigeration is greatly reduced.

A less expensive method of cooling a church consists of the installation of exhaust fans in the walls near the roof. If the windows are opened near the ground and these exhaust fans are turned on during the night, they will force out the hot, stale air and suck in the cool night air. The windows can be closed and the fans stopped early the next morning, and the building will be comparatively cool during the morning worship service.

AIR CONDITIONING

The foregoing are means of merely cooling a church building and should not be thought of as methods of air conditioning. Cooling is just one phase of air conditioning, which may be defined as the artificial control of the humidity, temperature, motion, and purity of the air within buildings.

Churches with forced-air heating systems have found these easily adaptable to air conditioning, since all that must be added is some apparatus for purifying, cooling, and humidifying the air, which has already been drawn in through inlets in the walls.

Some churches find it satisfactory to install small, mobile air conditioning units. These are effective in small rooms, and

161

GLASS BLOCKS IN CHURCH CONSTRUCTION

St. Mary's Episcopal Church, Eugene, Oreg.

Glass blocks are used in both the windows and the tower of this church in the Northwest. Use of this glass in church construction is new but is being increasingly considered for its beauty, utility, and insulating qualities.

several types will cool and wash the air in fairly large churches. The tendency in the larger churches, however, is to establish permanent air conditioning plants.

Whether churches should specify air conditioning in their buildings will depend largely on whether they wish to hold services during the summer. There is a good basis for believing that if churches would follow the example of the motion-picture theaters, they could have good congregations throughout the warm months of the year. Mechanical air

162

Photograph by courtesy of Bruce Studios

THE MODERN TREND

Church of the Good Shepherd, Queens Village, N. Y.

Both exterior and interior show a decided trend to modernism. Yet the total impression is pleasing and worshipful.

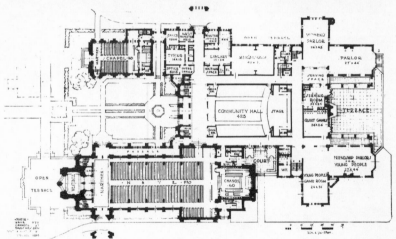

Wenner & Fink, Architects

A Modern City Church
Asbury First Methodist Church, Rochester, N. Y.

This great building will offer complete facilities for worship, education, and social life. It is built on a lot four and one-half acres in size and will provide parking space for 150 cars.

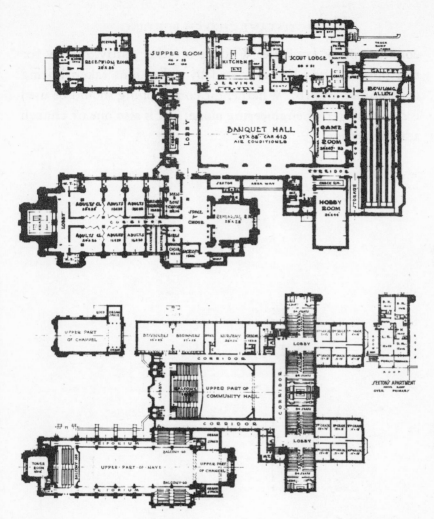

Wenner & Fink, Architects

A MODERN CITY CHURCH

Asbury First Methodist Church, Rochester, N. Y.

The educational and social rooms are very complete. Notice the series of departmental chapels on the second floor, also the number of serving rooms. The scout lodge has log walls and contains an open fireplace.

-conditioning is available. While it is rather costly, money for this purchase can be liquidated by collections taken during the summer months. Whether air conditioning should be used is not a matter of engineering alone, but is also one of church administration.

CHAPTER XIII

The Church Lawn

THOUSANDS of people look upon a church exterior for each individual who enters to worship. The properly designed church carries a constant message to these thousands. When the building is situated on well-kept grounds, the appearance of the property is more valuable than any new space which may be purchased. The wise church will see to it that its towers, windows, and walls are displayed to the best advantage.

A large building requires a large building lot. Unfortunately in our great cities the church lawn has too often been crowded out by encroaching neighbors and by the expansion of the church building. The ideal situation is to have the church building at such a distance from the street that a beautifully kept lawn is spread between it and the sidewalk.

The lawn of the Christ Lutheran Church, St. Paul, Minnesota, is a fine example of beautification of a church lot in an open space crowded by city business buildings. It has been transformed into the Overwick Memorial Chapel Garden. In this pleasant place one finds marble benches, flowing fountains, and blossoming flowers. A central position is given to a marble statue of Christ.

If a church has no land for lawn or park, the least it can

167

do is to keep the entire exterior of its building clean and attractive. The church steps can present an invitation to one who would worship. There may be a handrail for the aged and others who need it. An attractive announcement board, with its message brightly told with clean letters, may be erected. And, if possible, the pleasant notes of the chimes of a tower or an amplified organ broadcast at suitable periods.

The Court Street Christian Church, Salem, Oregon, had an abandoned church basement which invited refuse and got it. A minister with some vision thought that it might make an attractive garden spot. It was cleaned out. Vines were set next to the walls, and flowers were planted. Benches were installed. Soon it became a place of beauty and was called the Garden of Prayer.

In the warm summer days churches have found that a shaded spot out of doors makes a good meeting place for a restless class of boys and girls. It does not take much to prepare such a spot for the class. There should be shade, a little seclusion, and proper seats. If there is a somewhat concealed spot large enough for a picnic, an open-air fireplace is a splendid investment in sociability.

For churches which may wish to do so there is an opportunity to develop a Bible Garden, in which may be planted flowers and shrubs mentioned in the Bible. There are hundreds of these available which will grow well in American soil. For the person who may wish to follow this project, the volume *Bible Plants for American Gardens* by Eleanor S. King (The Macmillan Company) can be recommended. What better way is there of teaching the natural history of

USING THE OUT-OF-DOORS

The upper picture shows the fireplace, which is the center of the summer
social activities at the Baptist Church, Factoryville, Penn.

The lower picture reveals the attractive Bible garden at the Church
of the Wayfarer, Carmel-by-the-Sea, Calif. The bench at the entrance
has the invitation to "Rest and Be Thankful."

OPEN-AIR PULPIT
Westwood Community Methodist Church, Los Angeles, Calif.

MEMORIAL CHAPEL GARDEN
Christ Lutheran Church, St. Paul, Minn.

It is unusual to find a pleasant spot such as this near the busy city street. Churches which have areas of this kind can make them most inviting.

the Holy Land than to have a garden of vegetation from that land about the class as it studies?

The lawn may have a practical worship use. Among the churches which have included an open-air pulpit in their permanent architecture is the Westwood Community Methodist Church of Los Angeles, California. With seats placed on the lawn, the evening vespers of the warm months may be held in the open air.

Open-air gatherings on the church lawn have been common from early years. Festivals, sociables, and games have had their places. Even a church as crowded as Riverside Church of New York City has preserved an open-air court

171

where, at the proper times, strawberry and other festivals are held.

Proper landscaping of church exteriors costs money. But the expense is small compared with that of building construction. Also, here is a place where voluntary services may be used. Under the direction of the proper person amateur lovers of plants and of the out-of-doors may build their personalities into the church.

While the development of the out-of-doors has not been entirely unexplored, a great many churches have never used the opportunities they have close at hand for beautifying their property. A little direction and money can give meaning to the Bible verse: "Worship the Lord in the beauty of holiness."

CHAPTER XIV

The Parsonage

PARSONAGE, rectory, or manse—the name varies with the denomination. But each name means the same thing. It is a home for the minister.

All of the arguments seem to be in favor of a church's providing a parsonage. It makes it easy for the minister to come into a community with assurance that he has a place for his family. It assures the church that the pastor is conveniently located. It helps quiet the conscience of the church when the minister's home is usurped for social gatherings. The fact that the church provides it gives the people an interest in the building.

The courts have recognized that the relationship of a pastor to the parsonage he occupies is quite different from that of a tenant to rented quarters. State laws often provide tax exemption for the parsonage.[1] The legal basis of tax exemption is that it is necessary to house the minister near the church so that he may properly perform his duties. In some states

[1] The following states allow all or part tax exemption on parsonages, rectories, and manses: Connecticut (up to $5,000); District of Columbia; Florida; Kansas; Kentucky (½ acre in city, 2 acres in country); Louisiana; Maine (up to $6,000); Maryland; Michigan; Missouri; New Hampshire (up to $2,500); New Jersey ($5,000 value, 5 acres of ground); New York (up to $2,000); North Carolina; North Dakota; South Carolina; Virginia; Washington (if parsonage is on church site); West Virginia; Wisconsin; Wyoming. In some other states which do not specifically give exemption by law the local tax assessors may grant exemption.

173

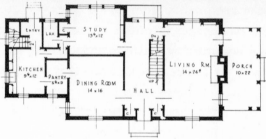

· FIRST · FLOOR · PLAN ·

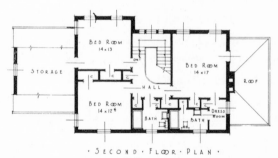

· SECOND · FLOOR · PLAN ·

THE PARSONAGE

This is a substantial and attractive building of Colonial design. The study on the first floor may be reached from the center hall without disturbing members of the family. There is also a convenient back entrance.

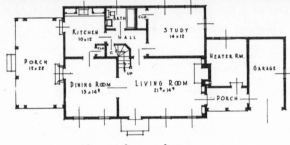

· FIRST · FLOOR · PLAN ·

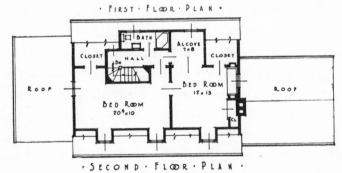

· SECOND · FLOOR · PLAN ·

Department of Church Architecture,
Baptist Sunday School Board, Nashville, Tenn.

THE PARSONAGE

The Cape Cod design on this page is less expensive. The study is not as well protected. But it is a pleasant home and has individuality. Both homes provide adequate bath facilities.

there is a distinction between the parsonage which adjoins the church and the one which is situated at a distance. A recent court decision held that the exemption of taxation on the parsonage was available only when, by reason of proximity to the church, it provided a convenient access to the minister.

When a minister receives a salary plus parsonage, he is not required to report the rental value of the parsonage on his income tax. When, in lieu of a parsonage, he receives additional cash compensation, the amount so received is taxable.

As a rule the parsonage should be built near the church. Like the church, the minister should be identified with the community he serves. There are of course situations where, for practical reasons, this is not advisable. There are crowded city areas where room is not available for a parsonage next to the church. The church then must provide office space, so that the minister is associated with the church.

When the church furnishes an office for the minister, is it wise that the parsonage be so constructed that he also has a study in his home? If so, this means building an additional room. This room should be situated near an entrance, so that visitors may enter and leave without passing through the family rooms. There will be visitors who do not come to pay social visits, but who wish to confer with the pastor. The minister's study, like the doctor's office, should encourage callers who need the help the minister has to give.

The parsonage should have plenty of sleeping rooms. There will be guests when visiting ministers come to the parish, when denominational officials make their visits, or when missionaries speak to the church. Inasmuch as there are

176

resources available, there should be hospitality in the parsonage. To give every comfort to the guest, additional toilet facilities should be close to the guest room.

The living room, dining room, and kitchen of the parsonage should be larger than those necessary for the requirements of an ordinary small family. There will be social and religious gatherings in the home, and the additional room will come in handy. When a half-dozen women are getting a meal in the kitchen, the most efficient kitchenette will be too crowded.

Additional rooms means more expense in the upkeep. The cost of building maintenance should fall upon the church instead of the minister. I might add, though it is outside of the scope of this book, that it would be well if the church also assumed a portion of the fuel, electric light, and water bills.

The church has the obligation to keep the parsonage in first-class condition, even as it keeps the church in such condition. The minister has the obligation to use the property with courtesy and care. When these mutual obligations are observed, both church and minister should profit from the erection of a parsonage.

Glossary

AISLE: Passageway through the nave in the direction of the length of the building.

ALTAR: The place reserved for the sacrament of the Lord's Supper.

ALTAR CLOTH: The white "fair linen" cloth which covers the altar.

ALTAR CROSS: A cross of wood or metal which is suspended over the altar or placed upon it.

ALTAR LIGHTS: Candles placed on the altar, including the two eucharistic candles usually used.

ANTEPENDIUM: A hanging at the front of the pulpit. Usually embroidered with an appropriate symbol.

APSE: The semi-circular or polygonal projection of the east end of a church building in which the Lord's Table is placed.

BAPTISTRY: That part of the building which contains the baptismal font or the pool.

BASILICA: An oblong assembly hall.

CANDELABRUM (plural, Candelabra): An ornamental branch candlestick.

CHALICE: The cup in which the sacramental wine is consecrated.

CHANCEL: That part of the building which contains the sanctuary and its approaches; it may also contain the choir, the pulpit, the lectern, and the font.

CHOIR: That part of the building in which the seats for the singers are located.

CHOIR STALLS: Benches placed in the choir to accommodate the singers.

CLERGY STALLS: Chairs or benches placed in the chancel for the use of the clergy.

CREDENCE: A shelf or table placed near the altar to hold the eucharistic vessels, the alms basin, and offering plates.

CRUCIFIX: A cross bearing a figure in the likeness of the body of Christ. Not common in Protestant churches, where a plain cross is usually preferred.

CRUCIFORM: A type of church building constructed in the form of a cross.

CUP: The chalice or its sacramental contents.

DOSSAL or DORSAL: An ornamental curtain which covers the wall back and above the altar.

EAST: The liturgical east is that part of the building in which the Lord's Table is located.

ELEMENTS: The materials used in the sacraments: bread, wine or water.

EUCHARISTIC LIGHTS: The two candles first placed on the altar.

FAIR LINEN: See altar cloth.

FONT: Stationary vessel used to hold water for the sacrament of baptism.

FRONTAL: A covering over the front of the altar.

GRADINE: A little step or retable rising above the altar and to the back of it. Flowers are placed on the retable, not usually on the altar.

HOLY TABLE: Altar or Lord's Table.

LECTERN: A reading desk from which the Scriptures are read.

LITANY DESK: The prayer desk from which the litany and confession may be said.

LORD'S TABLE: Altar or Holy Table.

MISSAL STAND: A small wooden or metal stand placed on the altar to hold the prayer book.

NARTHEX: The vestibule or foyer of the church.

NAVE: The part of the church set apart for the worshiping congregation.

ORNAMENTS: Accessories or decorations used in the chancel.

PALL: The linen cloth, or linen-covered square of cardboard with which the chalice is covered.

PASCHAL CANDLESTICK: Large candle holder for the Paschal or Easter Candle.

PATEN: Shallow dish on which the communion bread is placed.

PEDENTIVE: Vaulting.

PULPIT: The place in or near the chancel from which the sermon is preached.

PYX: A vessel in which the sacrament is reserved.

REREDOS: Carved wall or screen in back of the altar.

RETABLE: See Gradine.

ROOD: A cross or crucifix.

ROOD BEAM: A beam spanning the church and separating the chancel from the nave.

SACISTRY: A room, near the chancel, where the sacred vessels are kept, and where the clergy prepare themselves for their devotions.

180

SANCTUARY. That part of the church in which is the altar, usually at the east of the chancel.

SUPER-FRONTAL: A short hanging used to cover the upper part of the frontal.

TAPER: A waxed candle.

TRANSEPT: Space between the pews and the steps of the chancel; in a cruciform church, the arms of the cross.

VEIL: The fine linen cloth used to cover the sacramental vessels.

Bibliography

Anderson, Martin. *Planning and Financing the New Church*. Augsburg
 Publishing House, Minneapolis, 1944. 80 pages. Largely a book of well
 selected plans for modern churches. Sketchy but valuable.
Connick, Charles J. *Adventure in Light and Color*. Random House, New
 York, 1937. 428 pages. An authoritative volume on glass and color.
Conover, Elbert M. *Building the House of God*. Methodist Book Concern,
 1928. A very useful survey of the field by the director of the Interde-
 nominational Bureau of Architecture.
 Church Building Finance. Interdenominational Bureau of Architecture,
 1946. 62 pages. Well illustrated.
 Planning the Small Church. Interdenominational Bureau of Architec-
 ture. 44 pages. Well illustrated.
 Rebuilding the Town and Country Church. Interdenominational Bureau
 of Architecture. 16 pages. Well illustrated.
 Building for Worship. Interdenominational Bureau of Architecture. 62
 pages. Well illustrated.
 Building and Equipment for Religious Education. Interdenominational
 Bureau of Architecture. 54 pages. Well illustrated.
 Planning Church Buildings. Interdenominational Bureau of Architec-
 ture. Plans of churches costing from $30,000 to $850,000. 64 pages.
 Well illustrated.
 The Church Building Guide. Interdenominational Bureau of Architec-
 ture. Covers all phases of promotion and building. 158 pages. Well illus-
 trated.
 These booklets may be ordered from the Interdenominational Bureau of
Architecture, 297 Fourth Ave., New York 10, N. Y.
Cram, Ralph Adams. *Church Building*. Marshall Jones, Boston, 1914. 344
 pages. An authoritative book but unfortunately out of print. Cram was
 a leader in the revival of the Gothic.
*Drummond, Andrew Langdale. *Church Architecture of Protestantism*.
 Charles Scribner's Sons, New York, 1935. 344 pages. Probably the best
 survey of Protestant building. Written by a Scotsman. Much of the
 material deals with American churches.

Leach, William H. *The Altar in Your Church*. Goodenough & Woglom Company, New York. Well illustrated.

Powys, A. R. *The English Parish Church*. Longmans, Green and Co., New York, 1930. 165 pages. A pocket sized volume which traces the rise and development of the English church architecture.

Scotford, John R. *The Church Beautiful*. The Pilgrim Press, Boston, 1945. 161 pages. As the name implies, it is a volume with ideas for making the church beautiful. Worth while for clergy and laymen.

Short, Ernest H. *A History of Religious Architecture*. Macmillan, New York, 1925. 344 pages. Another one of the good books which has gone out of print.

Speare, Eva A. *Colonial Meeting Houses of New Hampshire Compared With Their Contemporaries in New England*. Daughters of Colonial Wars, State of New Hampshire, Plymouth, N. H., 1938. 213 pages. An intriguing book with many photographic illustrations.

Stafford, Thomas Albert. *Christian Symbolism in the Evangelical Churches*. Abingdon-Cokesbury, 1942. 217 pages. A popular reference book on religious symbolism.

*Vogt, Von Ogden. *Art and Religion*. Yale University Press, 1929. 263 pages. Still the best volume in its particular field.

Webber, Frederick R. *Church Symbolism*. Jansen Publishing Company, Cleveland, Ohio, 1938. 419 pages. This book is the accepted authority on religious symbolism.

The Small Church: How to Build and Furnish It. Jansen Publishing Company, Cleveland, Ohio, 1937. 315 pages. Shows that small churches can combine beauty and utility.

Index of Churches Shown in the Illustrations

185.

INDEX

General Index

Acoustics, correcting the, 145
Address system, 145-46
Age groups, building for, 116-25
Air conditioning, 161-66
Altar, 88-94, 97
  ornaments, 97
Architect, the
  fees, 34-37
  selecting, 32-37
Architecture, types of
  Apostolic churches, 81
  Basilican churches, 81-82
  Byzantine, 82
  Colonial, 83
  Gothic, 82
  Renaissance, 83
  Romanesque, 82
Auxiliary features, 135-36

Baptistry, 98
Bible Plants for American Gardens, 168
Building committee, organization of, 23-24
Building fund
  campaign, planning the, 40-48, 55-58
  canvass, how to conduct, 53-55
  segregation of, 66, 68
  size of the, 39-40, 45-48, 54-48

Cathedral of St. John the Divine, New York City, 150
Chancel, the, 88-98
Church Architectural Guild, 32
Church of the Abiding Presence, Gettysburg, Penn., 108
Classrooms, 118-23
Comity, 16
Communion table, 88, 97
Conover, Dr. Elbert M., 18
Cooling, methods of, 160-61
Court Street Christian Church, Salem, Oreg., 168

Court Street Methodist Church, Rockford, Ill., 141
Cram, Ralph Adams, 85-86

Departmental assemblies, 123-25
Dramatization and pageantry, 111-13, 133-34
Drummond, A. L., 77

Education, visual, 111, 136
Educational program in church building, 17-18

Federation, church, as source of information, 16
Fellowship hall, 129
Financing
  annuities, 69-72
  insurance, 72-73
  pledges, 60-62, 65
  professional fund raisers, 41-42, 48
  securities as gifts, 65
  solicitation from classes, 53
  surveys, 14, 16-17
  war bonds as gifts, 65
Furnishings, church, 98-103

Gardens, Bible, 168
Gredler, John G., 39-40
Guidance, denominational, 27, 34, 50-52

Heating, 156-59
  hot air, 156-57
  radiation, 157-58
  steam, 156-57
Hobby and club rooms, 115

Indebtedness, liquidation of, 72-73
Interdenominational Bureau of Architecture, 17

Kitchen, 130-32
Kitchenettes, 132

187

INDEX